THE ANGLO-NORWEGIAN FISHERIES CASE OF 1951 AND THE CHANGING LAW OF THE TERRITORIAL SEA

by Teruo Kobayashi

University of Florida Monographs

SOCIAL SCIENCES
No. 26, Spring 1965

UNIVERSITY OF FLORIDA PRESS / GAINESVILLE, FLORIDA

ACKNOWLEDGMENTS

I am deeply indebted to Professor Oscar Svarlien of the University of Florida for putting his profound scholarship in the field of international law at my disposal; for his illuminating guidance, from which I first gained my interest and knowledge in the present study; and for his generous advice and encouragement which have enabled me to complete this work. I am also grateful to Professor Frederick H. Hartmann also of the University of Florida who offered his time and cooperation in directing and criticizing my first draft at the doctoral dissertation stage. I wish to thank especially Professor Nathan Smith, my former associate and the chairman of the Department of History and Political Science at Washington College, for his counsel and friendship, for his careful scrutinizing of the draft, and for his elaborate comments in the final preparation of this manuscript. His service has been indispensable.

My appreciation is extended also to the following people for help in many important ways: Professor C. H. M. Waldock of Oxford University and the late S. Whittemore Boggs for their generosity in offering me their invaluable works in the field of the law of the territorial sea; Professors Manning J. Dauer, Ernest R. Bartley, and John Harrison, of the University of Florida, and also Professor Alfred Diamant of Haverford College, for their scholarly suggestions and reading of my dissertation; Mr. George Worsley of the International Law Association and Dr. Sompong Sucharitkul of the International Commission of Jurists at the Hague, for their suggestions on numerous materials for research.

Thanks also are due the Graduate School of the University of Florida for making possible the publication of the Monograph.

I am happy to acknowledge the service of my parents, and particularly to thank my wife, Natsue, for her untiring companionship and her typing of all the drafts.

TERUO KOBAYASHI

ELMIRA, NEW YORK
MARCH, 1965

CONTENTS

1. INTRODUCTION

The oceans which cover nearly three-quarters of the earth have long been the highways of commerce and intercourse between nations. Over many centuries the peoples of the world have developed through usage a common law of the sea. Many elements of the law grew out of ancient custom and traditional use of the sea, greatly influenced by the attitudes of important maritime powers or those struggling to attain this status. Political and economic necessities dominated the views of these states, causing them to disagree endlessly with one another about the nature and content of the slowly developing and imperfect international law of the sea.

Ever since the time of Hugo Grotius—and even before—there has been diplomatic disagreement and sometimes resort to arms over such issues as the baseline from which the extent of the territorial sea should be measured, the width of this sea itself, and the freedom of the high seas.

With the beginning of the nineteenth century and the move toward industrialization, debate over these and allied questions increased. New problems evolved, born of nations increasingly bound together by technology and communication in a world lacking a corresponding community consciousness. By the middle of the twentieth century national claims of seaward jurisdiction had become unprecedentedly numerous, varied, and inconsistent. Never, for states facing the high seas, has there been so great a need for coastal-sea area limitations which could be universally or at least generally accepted.

Without determined efforts to resolve these problems, the situation could readily lead to constantly increasing international friction. Mutual distrust, a compelling desire for security, interest in the rights of navigation by sea and by air, a sense of the need to conserve fish and mineral resources in and under the sea, the hope of increased revenues, simple jingoistic feeling—all these drives and others contribute to mounting tension. A unique source of contention in modern times has been the expansion of international law from that of the small family of nations in which it arose into a law that is world-wide. The law today claims the allegiance of nations which had no part in building it up, and which have never known or no longer accept the fundamental beliefs and sentiments on which it was originally founded. At least some of these nations are inclined to look upon international law as an alien system which the

1

Western nations, whose moral or intellectual leadership they no longer recognize, are trying to impose upon them, and in effect they have begun to claim the right to select from among its rules only those which suit their needs and interests. Even among the Western nations there has been increased tendency to criticize and protest the conservative nature of traditional international law, which is often found lacking perspective in terms of time and circumstances which have changed rapidly.[1]

The clash between swiftly changing national interests and practices regarding the sea and customary rules that no longer suit the circumstances has created controversies that have yet to be fully settled. To reach possible agreement on the questions of territorial sea baseline and extent, it is necessary to discard the strait jacket of abstract doctrine and "pure" juridical formulation. Inflexible and conservative approaches to international law which ignore the realities of the modern situation will not do. Workable rules for the conduct of states must have regard for their interests and practices in accordance with changes in time and circumstances.

A realistic approach toward a solution came from the International Court of Justice which on December 18, 1951 pronounced judgment in a particular dispute involving problems of the sea: the *Anglo-Norwegian Fisheries Case*.[2] The dispute involved the Norwegian system of delimiting the territorial sea by a "straight baseline" method, according to which the four-mile extent of the territorial sea is calculated from imaginary baselines drawn between the headlands of bays and all the Norwegian fjords on the mainland and between the most extreme of islands, islets, and reefs. What was involved in the dispute was not only the magnified extent of the Norwegian territorial sea through the use of this method, but more significantly the fundamental philosophies behind the diametrically opposed viewpoints of the two parties as to the nature and problems of the territorial sea in general: Great Britain held fast to the more or less traditional philosophy based on the rigid application of the general rules allegedly favorable to the wider extent of freedom of the sea, with a strictly limited exception for historic titles; while Norway advocated the modern trends of international law, particularly in-

1. Quincy Wright, "The Role of Law," in *Organizing Peace in the Nuclear Age* (New York: Commission to Study the Organization of Peace, 1959), p. 34.

2. International Court of Justice, *Fisheries Case (United Kingdom v. Norway) Judgment of 18 December 1951: Reports of Judgments, Advisory Opinions and Orders*; hereafter cited as I.C.J., *Reports*. The written and oral proceedings and accompanying materials are in International Court of Justice, *Fisheries Case (United Kingdom v. Norway) Judgment of 18 December 1951: Pleadings, Oral Arguments, Documents*; hereafter cited as I.C.J., *Pleadings*.

2

sisting on a flexible application to specific cases of the general rules of international law.

The Court's decision, under a rather inclusive general rule, the "general direction of the coast," in favor of the Norwegian contentions transcended in its significance, therefore, the particular dispute involved and the interests of the parties. The defeat of Great Britain, traditionally one of the leading maritime powers, alone merits one's attention. Undoubtedly it opened new prospects, if not Pandora's box, for the future development of international law.[3] A salient point in the case is that the decision was made between the conflicting interests and views of two of the "old" Western nations, at the time when there still were few independent African and Asian nations in the world community. The great significance of the decision made it inevitable that it would be the subject of passionate attention and continuing debate.[4]

The Anglo-Norwegian Fisheries Case can be understood only in a double perspective: It must be seen in the light of both the preceding development of the law of the sea which the Court appraised and its subsequent impact on state practices and on current law trends. Thus the focus of this study is on the case as a transition step in the evolution of the law of the territorial sea. Of the many aspects of the law touched upon in the case, we shall concentrate on the relationship between the freedom of the high seas and the limitations of the territorial sea, involving the extent of seaward jurisdiction and how to measure or delimit it.

3. Strictly speaking, the judgment could not be a precedent in the Anglo-American sense of *stare decisis*. By Article 59 of the Statutes of the I.C.J., "The decision of the Court has no binding force except between the parties and in respect to that particular case." But despite these provisions, the Court's decisions are widely regarded as authoritative in declaring what the law is.

4. See Brierly, *Law of Nations*, p. 175; Lauterpacht, "Freedom of the Seas"; Waldock, "Fisheries Case"; Evensen, "Fisheries Case" (short-title citations are used for secondary sources; see the Bibliography for full bibliographical information).

2. THE LAW OF THE
TERRITORIAL SEA IN FLUX

It is universally recognized that the high seas are not susceptible to territorial appropriation, that they are free and open to all nations. This principle of the freedom of the high seas is by no means absolute or self-contained. It has as its counterpart the principle of the territorial sea: certain areas of the sea adjacent to coasts belong to the coastal states and thus are subject to their sovereign rights. A major portion of the law of the seas has, in fact, centered around two perennial questions concerning the proper or equitable relationship between these principles. How far out in the ocean lies the line of demarcation between the high seas and the territorial sea? How should this line of demarcation be determined and drawn? Resolution of these questions has been vital to a harmonious relationship between the interests of nations as a community and their exclusive interests.

In the past, an answer to these essential questions, in the form of a balance of conflicting national interests, tied up as it was with the problems of national defense, oceanic and coastal fisheries, navigation, and other economic and social interests, was provided by international law. The great maritime powers, as is understandable, controlled the establishment of precedent-making custom in the evolution of the international law of the sea. By the middle of the nineteenth century they considered that most of the outstanding problems had been settled.

Whatever satisfactory balance had been achieved, however, was strongly menaced by the technological and scientific developments resulting from the industrial revolution, the expanded economic interests of the coastal states in their use of the sea, and the rapidly changing political configuration of the world community, all of which made their greatest impact in the last half of the nineteenth century. The trend thereafter has been toward expansion of the seaward jurisdictions of the coastal states. Recent developments have pushed the line of demarcation seaward, into what had been traditionally considered the realm of the high seas. This has challenged the scope of application of the principle of freedom of the seas, if not the doctrine itself.

FREEDOM OF THE SEAS AND THE TERRITORIAL SEA

Already in Roman times there was a concept that the sea was free to the common use of all men, although Roman jurisprudence did not de-

4

velop any notion of international law in the modern sense.[1] Not until Roman law had been adapted to the practical needs of the Middle Ages was the creation of a legal theory defining the international status of the sea undertaken. Probably as incidental to the king's *Regalia* during feudalism, some jurists in the fourteenth century seriously considered a legal relationship between the high seas open to all and sovereign rights over adjacent waters. They were prompted mainly by the exigencies of their age—the need for policing the sea to suppress piracy and to make it safe for navigation and commerce.[2]

With the end of the Middle Ages came the era of *dominium maris*. Maritime powers, such as Spain and Portugal, began to claim proprietary rights over the vast seas and oceans of the world. Great changes in the world situation affected the problems of the sea: the discovery of a new hemisphere, the rapid increase in world population, the rise of maritime powers in the west of Europe, the expansion of commercial fisheries, the ambitions of self-conscious monarchs and the resulting conflicts of their aspirations to extend their domain, both to land and sea.[3]

For some time this bold assumption of *dominium maris* passed without formal challenge. But finally, despite her obvious inconsistency,[4] Great Britain stoutly protested the pretentious claims of Spain and Portugal. Queen Elizabeth was perhaps the first to assert in actual diplomacy the modern concept of the freedom of the seas. She proclaimed in 1580: "The use of the sea and air is common to all; neither can any title to the ocean belong to any people or private man."[5] It is clear, however, that her opposition to the Iberian kings' claims was based less on principle than on her desire to break the Iberian monopoly of the sea.

A real legal defense of the freedom of the seas came from Hugo Grotius in his work *Mare Liberum* (1609). Grotius asserted that the freedom of navigation on the high seas is the "most specific and unimpeachable axiom of the Law of Nations" and "self-evident and immutable." More precisely, he wrote that "the sea is a thing so clearly common to all" that "no part of the sea can be considered as the territory of any people whatsoever." Important in this connection was Gro-

---

1. Fenn, *Right of Fishery*, pp. 21-22, on the opinions of Justinian, Ulpian, and Paulus.
2. Fenn, pp. 94, 97-98, 102, 108-9, 124-25, on the opinions of Bartolus de Sasoferrato, Baldus de Ubaldi, and Albericus Gentilis.
3. See Svarlien, *Law of Nations*, p. 185.
4. Smith, *Great Britain and the Law of Nations*, II, 113.
5. Smith, *Law and Custom*, p. 44.

tius' inclusion of the freedom of fishing: "now the same principle which applies to navigation applies also to fishing, namely, that it remains free and open to all."[6] Grotius' definition of the freedom of the seas pointed out the British inconsistency. The British had combined their interests in freedom of navigation with a concern to preserve their own monopoly of fishing in the vicinity of their shores, as can be seen in the prohibition issued against Dutch fishermen by James I in 1609.

Grotius met vigorous objections from the British jurists, so far as the freedom of fishing was concerned. William Welwood claimed that the relation of the land to the adjacent sea was so intimate that the ruler of the land must not alienate any part of the sea, or any use of it, for the welfare of his people.[7] Welwood may have been the first author who clearly enunciated the need for the principle of the territorial sea, according to which the inhabitants of a country had a primary and exclusive right to the fisheries along its coasts.[8] John Selden in 1663 elaborated on Welwood's theme. Although his claims to the sea were more sweeping than most that would be made in the future, he did make the sound point that there was nothing in the nature of the sea to prevent its appropriation or the claim of sovereign rights over it.[9]

In this "battle of the books" was obviously the beginning of the controversy over the relationship between the freedom of the seas and the territorial sea. It is important to remember that behind this battle were the conflicting national interests of the maritime powers. The nations were unwilling to accept the ideas that the free and common seas touched their very shores and that all nations could fish along the shores or could hold naval battles so close as to threaten the peace and order of a neutral nation. Nor could they find it practical to allow or make claims of dominion over vast ocean areas, which would prevent free navigation and fishing on the high seas. The Thirty Years' War gave particular impetus to the need of neutrals to protect their coastal seas from becoming the scene of battle. By the Peace of Westphalia in 1648, both freedom of the seas and the territorial sea already existed in practical fact; the doctrines justifying the fact were born out of "a convenient compromise between conflicting interests" at that time.[10]

In practice the British naval power played the most important role in strengthening these principles. With victory over the Spanish Armada in 1588, Britain became the world's leading naval power, with the abil-

6. *Freedom of the Seas*, pp. 7, 34, 32 (order of quotations).
7. *Abridgement of All Sea-Lawes*, pp. 199-201, 202.
8. Fulton, *Sovereignty of the Sea*, p. 357n.
9. *Mare Clausum*, cited in Fenn, p. 219.
10. Jessup, *Law of Territorial Waters*, p. 7.

ity to mold maritime law in significant degree. At the same time, her oceanic fisheries and commerce became so extensive that it suited her interest to keep the territorial belts of other nations as narrow as possible and to magnify freedom of navigation.[11] Thus the doctrine of the freedom of the seas was truly "the result of a marriage of laissez-faire economics to British gunboats."[12] It may not be incorrect therefore to say that the question of relationship between the high seas and the territorial sea was largely "a problem for diplomacy rather than for law."[13]

THE SEAWARD JURISDICTIONS

A more crucial problem in the relationship between the high seas and the territorial sea is the line of demarcation between the two. Unless the line is definitely understood and drawn, neither principle will be clearly defined. In recent times this problem has become more complex than ever by the appearance of the concepts of the contiguous zone, the continental shelf, and fishery conservation or monopoly.

The Territorial Sea.—Generally Cornelius van Bynkershoek is credited with the origin of the cannon-shot rule. He asserted in 1702 that "the dominion of the land ends where the power of arms ends" or "so far as cannon balls are projected."[14] Since the range of guns, actually placed on the shore, was approximately three miles or one marine league in the eighteenth century, the cannon-shot rule came to be equated with the three-mile limit of the territorial sea. The rule originated among the Mediterranean states to safeguard neutrality.[15] Recent research, however, seems to indicate that the present three-mile limit derived not only from the cannon-shot rule, but also from the Scandinavian concept of a "continuous belt" of the coastal waters measured from the shoreline.[16]

Even prior to Bynkershoek's time, the doctrine of a territorial continuous belt along the coast had been put into practice by the Danes and Norwegians. Although they made claims to *dominium maris* in the Northern Seas during the sixteenth century, they retreated gradually to a claim of one Scandinavian league (approximately four nautical miles) off the coast. Their purpose was to protect their primary economic interests (coastal fisheries) and their neutrality against increasing pressure from Great Britain and France. By the Decree of 1598, for ex-

11. Riesenfeld, *Protection of Fisheries*, pp. 21-22; see also Higgins and Colombos, *Law of the Sea*, 1945, pp. 35-36, 41, 45-47.
12. Kaplan and Katzenbach, *Political Foundation*, p. 147.
13. Fenn, *Right of Fishery*, p. 220.
14. *De dominio maris*, p. 44.
15. Jessup, *Law of Territorial Waters*, pp. 5-7; see also Marsden, *Documents Relating to Law*, I, 487.
16. Walker, "Territorial Waters," pp. 211-12; Waldock, "International Law."

7

ample, Denmark reserved to its subjects alone the fisheries off Iceland within a belt of two leagues from the coasts of the island, and finally the limit was contracted to one league in 1832.[17] By the end of the eighteenth century, the continuous belt and cannon-shot were brought together in a compromise, a continuous belt three miles in extent.[18] The three-mile limit, however, never crystallized into any hard and fast rule of international law. The concept of the limit, which was generally a convenient compromise of conflicting national interests, was increasingly adapted to changed conditions during the nineteenth century, and as one authority noted, gave way still more recently to the conviction that it did not conform to actual international practice at all.[19] First, the increased range and more accurate aim of artillery threatened the national security interest in neutrality.[20] Second, the economic interests of the coastal states, especially fisheries, became increasingly affected by progress in technique and consequent increase in activities. The problem of fishery conservation became serious. In short, the three-mile limit was considered "obsolete and inadequate" for the protection of economic resources.[21] But no agreement on the proper extent of the territorial sea was ever reached.

The practice of states has been no less loosely fixed than the theory of the three-mile limit. The exception has been those great maritime powers, Great Britain, Germany, Japan, and the United States, which had a common interest in giving the widest scope to the freedom of the seas.[22] It is interesting to note that these four powers accounted for "nearly eighty per cent of the world's effective tonnage" in 1930.[23]

At the Hague Codification Conference of 1930, more than a majority of states present expressed serious concern in one way or another with

17. Kent, "Historical Origin"; Oscar Svarlien states that the introduction of the marine league dates back as far as 1743—"Territorial Sea," p. 337.
18. Jessup, *Law of Territorial Waters*, p. 7.
19. See Wilson, "Topic I," p. 15; Reeves, "Submarine and Innocent Passage," p. 148.
20. As early as 1785 George Friedrich von Martens wrote to this effect—see his *Law of Nations*, p. 160; see also Hall, *International Law*, p. 126; Svarlien, *Law of Nations*, p. 162.
21. Westlake, *International Law*, I, 185.
22. See Sorensen, "Law of the Sea," p. 199. For British practice, see Higgins and Colombos, *Law of the Sea*, 1945, pp. 65-66; the Territorial Waters Jurisdiction Act of 1878, 41 & 42 Vict. c. 73 (1878). For the U.S., Moore, *Digest*, I, 702-6. For Japan, Fulton, pp. 661-63; the *Tatsu Maru* case as cited in *American Journal of International Law*, II (1908), 391 (hereafter the *Journal* is cited as *A.J.I.L.*). For Germany see Great Britain, Foreign Office, *British and Foreign State Papers, 1914*, CVII, pt. I, 833. See also Appendices I and II, below.
23. Sir Maurice Gwyer in "League of Nations," *A.J.I.L.*, XXIV (1930), Supp. 254.

the inadequacy of the three-mile limit for protection of their respective interests, particularly coastal fisheries and national safety. The "varying geographical and economic conditions in different states and parts of the world" were considered important factors in the lack of uniformity of any definite territorial limit seaward.[24] On the whole "the Conference probably did more harm than good" to the three-mile limit by bringing into the open the varying practices of the states and their general dissatisfaction with the limit.[25] It was the major victim of the Conference and became a "dethroned idol."[76] Since then, particularly since 1945, the practices of states became increasingly expansive, creating further uncertainty. Some states have claimed even a 200-mile limit.[27] It can be stated, in conclusion, that there has been a rule of international law setting the minimum extent of the territorial sea, the three-mile limit, but not a generally recognized maximum.[28]

The Contiguous Zone.—The general admission that under modern conditions the three-mile limit is neither wide enough nor flexible enough to protect legitimate interests of the coastal states had led many states not only to outright expansion of their territorial sea but also to the often indeterminate concept of the contiguous zone. According to this concept, a coastal state may exercise certain rights for "protective" or "preventive" purposes over a certain portion of the high seas contiguous to its territorial sea.

Authorities have emphasized the legal distinction between the sovereign rights of a state over its territorial sea and its protective or preventive jurisdiction over the contiguous zone.[29] That is, rights based on sovereignty are generally considered absolute, whereas the rights of protective jurisdiction are "extraterritorial rights," limited and indefinite without changing the legal status of the high seas in the zone.[30] In practice, however, the contiguous zone has frequently resulted in extending the sovereign rights of the territorial sea to a new and wider dimension into the high seas, the protective jurisdiction in the end being converted into a more or less prohibitive jurisdiction.[31]

---

24. Reinkemeyer, *Die sowjetische Zwölfmeilenzone*, p. 235 (see pp. 136-39 for the Russian practice of a 12-mile zone as early as 1909); see Appendix I, below, for a synoptical table of 1930.
25. Brierly, *Law of Nations*, p. 81.
26. "Idole renversée," in Gidel, *Droit international*, III, 151.
27. See Appendix II, below.
28. Reeves, "Codification of the Law," p. 491; for the complexity of this matter, see Brierly, "Contiguous Zone," p. 157; Svarlien, "Territorial Sea," p. 344.
29. Hyde, *International Law*, I, 467.
30. Allen, "Territorial Waters," p. 479; Svarlien, "Territorial Sea," pp. 334-36.
31. Reeves, "Codification of the Law," p. 494; see Hackworth, *Digest*, I, 666-67,

Nevertheless, the various demands—economic, political, social, and defensive—have sustained the need for the contiguous zone, and its legal status has been established, although its "specific security rights," its purposes, and its extent have remained quite uncertain.[32]

Even Great Britain, the champion of the three-mile limit, found itself increasingly disenchanted with it and sought protection for some of its national interests in the contiguous zone concept. In fact, Great Britain was the pioneer in introducing this concept in the Hovering Acts of 1736, 1802, and 1825.[33] This legislation established the principle of a five-mile (later six-mile) distance from the coast for enforcement of customs and quarantine laws. This in effect was a clear admission that the happy medium of interests found generally in the three-mile limit did not protect British interests in prevention of smuggling and in enforcement of customs and sanitary regulations.[34]

The United States adopted the British principle of hovering legislation in an Act of Congress of March 2, 1799, which provided for a four-league contiguous zone.[35] Since the passage of the Anti-Smuggling Act of 1935, the United States has asserted jurisdiction over foreign vessels in four different zones adjacent to its coasts: (1) the three-mile limit of the territorial sea, (2) the four-league customs waters, (3) the liquor treaty zone of one hour's sailing distance from the coast, and (4) the customs-enforcement area.[36] The last zone is notable in that the Anti-Smuggling Act authorized the President of the United States to establish "customs enforcement areas" up to 50 nautical miles beyond the twelve-

for the *Reidun* case (14 F. Supp. 112 [1936])—a Norwegian ship was seized more than 500 but less than 600 miles from the U.S. coast for the alleged violation of Sec. 205 of the Anti-Smuggling Act of 1935.

32. See the 1956 report of the International Law Commission, as cited in *A.J.I.L.*, LI (1957), Supp. 240.

33. The Hovering Acts, 9 Geo. II, c. 35, Secs. 18, 22 (1736). The Act of 1764 extended the limit to 2 leagues (4 Geo. III, c. 15, Sec. 33); the Act of 1802 farther extended it to 8 leagues for smuggling (42 Geo. III, c. 82); the Act of 1825 set forth quarantine regulations within 2 leagues from the shore (4 Geo. IV, c. 78, Sec. 8); see also Sec. 179 of the Customs Consolidation Act of 1876 (39 & 40 Vict., c. 36).

34. Smith, *Law and Custom*, p. 18, notes that Great Britain has been "seriously embarrassed by her own record"; Briggs, *Law of Nations*, p. 374, considers that the Customs Consolidation Act of 1876, repealing the previous acts by providing the 3-mile limit of the territorial sea for all purposes, has not really abolished the contiguous zones; see Jessup, *Law of Territorial Waters*, p. 79.

35. 1 Stat. 627, 647, 670 (1799).

36. Briggs, p. 375; for a legal analysis see Jessup, "Anti-Smuggling Act," pp. 101-6; see the U.S.-British treaty on 1 hour's sailing distance, 43 Stat. 1761 (1924)—the same treaty was concluded by the U.S. with Germany, Sweden, Norway, Denmark, Italy, Panama, Spain, Cuba, France, Belgium, Japan, Poland, Greece, and Chile.

mile customs waters and 100 miles "in each lateral direction away from the place or the immediate area of the hovering."[37] Many states have followed these examples,[38] and the validity of hovering legislation and customs enforcement regulations over a wide area of the high seas has seldom been challenged.[39]

The concept of the contiguous zone has also been applied to neutrality purposes.[40] As weaponry advanced and naval warfare methods became more accurate, swift, and versatile, the three-mile limit was found insufficient for neutrality and national security.[41] One of the spectacular attempts at creating neutrality zones was embodied in the Declaration of Panama of 1939, a joint declaration of the American Republics, which established a neutrality zone extending approximately 300 miles from the coasts of the Western Hemisphere, with the exception of Canada.[42] Subsequently, the American Republics protested against the belligerent acts committed by the German battleship *Graf Von Spee* and the British actions in sinking that vessel within this vast neutrality zone.[43]

Although such a flagrant expansion of the contiguous zone might not be accepted, reasonable claims advanced on the ground of self-defense, based on the principle of inviolability of national territory, particularly in time of war, have been generally recognized.[44] Even in time of peace some jurisdictional claims over the high seas have been advanced and accepted in the name of security and national emergency.[45] Because of

---

37. 49 Stat. 517, c. 438 (1935); see Title 1, Sec. 1(a) of the Act.
38. See the Treaty of Helsingfors, signed August 19, 1925, by Germany, Denmark, Estonia, Finland, Latvia, Lithuania, Norway, Poland, the Free City of Danzig, and the Soviet Union; it provided for a 12-mile zone for the suppression of smuggling alcoholic liquors—League of Nations, *Treaty Series*, XLII, 75, 79; for other treaties and practices see Higgins and Colombos, *Law of the Sea*, 1945, p. 92.
39. See League of Nations, *Acts of the Conference for the Codification of International Law*, pp. 119-62; U.N. Gen. Ass., *Report of the International Law Commission*, 8th Sess., Appendix 11 (hereafter cited as *Report of I.L.C.*); Gidel, *Droit international*, III, 363, 372, 444-54, 474-89; see Appendix II, below, for the numerous examples of such practices.
40. See the *Virginius* case in Moore, *Digest*, II, 895, 980, 983.
41. Hackworth, *Digest*, I, 660-63; Brown "Protective Jurisdiction," pp. 112-16.
42. See "Consultative Meeting of Foreign Ministers of the American Republics," 1939.
43. *International Law Situations*, 1939, pp. 68-71; Great Britain, France, and Germany, respectively, countered that the assent of the belligerents was necessary before the 300-mile limit, not sanctioned by international law, would be applicable to them (pp. 71-78).
44. *Ibid.*, p. 80; see League of Nations, *Bases of Discussion Drawn up for the Conference by the Preparatory Committee*, pp. 22-23, for the practices of states.
45. For a peacetime security zone see the "Defensive Sea Areas" as established by the U.S. in the Executive Order of June 12, 1952; the principles underlying

11

the varied interests, needs, and circumstances for which the contiguous zones are established, however, their extent has never been uniformly settled. But it is significant that the seaward jurisdiction of the coastal states has been further enlarged with the appearance of this doctrine.

The Continental Shelf and Fishery Conservation.—The expansion of the seaward jurisdiction of the coastal states was further accelerated by the extension of economic activities on the high seas: the exploration and exploitation of mineral resources of the sea bed and subsoil of the high seas, particularly oil, and the conservation of fisheries in the superjacent waters. The initiative in this direction was taken by the United States, one of the staunchest advocates of the freedom of the sea and the three-mile limit. President Harry S. Truman issued on September 28, 1945, the Proclamation on the Continental Shelf. Reflecting interest in the abundant deposits of natural resources in the oceanic subsoil, this proclaimed that the continental shelf beneath the high seas but contiguous to the coasts of the United States must be regarded "as appertaining to the United States, and subject to its jurisdiction and control." It asserted the monopolistic right of the United States to the shelf on the ground that "these resources frequently form a seaward extension of the land-mass of the coastal nation and are thus naturally appurtenant to it." However, the proclamation did not purport to affect "the character as high seas of the waters above the continental shelf and the right of their free and unimpeded navigation."[46]

This action was immediately followed by comparable proclamations and enactments by several Latin American nations. Going beyond the United States, however, a further claim to sovereignty over the high seas above the continental shelf was advanced by Mexico, Argentina, Chile, Panama, Peru, Ecuador, Costa Rica, Honduras, and El Salvador.[47] The last five nations proclaimed a 200-mile "maritime jurisdiction" in addition to the doctrine of the continental shelf.

Sovereignty over the territorial sea was traditionally considered to include sovereignty over the sea bed and subsoil in that area.[48] But the

---

the order are self-defense and national emergency—*International Law Situations,* 1955, p. 390. Though different in nature, another interesting practice is the establishment of temporary security zones for atomic bomb testing—see McDougal and Schlei, "Hydrogen Bomb Tests," pp. 674-88.

46. 10 Fed. Reg. 12303 (1945), cited in Briggs, *Law of Nations,* pp. 378-79.

47. For texts of proclamations and enactments in addition to the above states, see *U.N. Legislative Series, Laws and Regulations on the Regime of the High Seas,* 1951, pp. 3-44, 47, 299-305; see Appendix II, below, for claims by others.

48. See the Cornwall Submarine Act of 1858, 21 & 22 Vict. c. 109 (1858); *U.S.* v. *California,* 232 U.S. 10, 38 (1947).

sovereignty of any state over the bed of the high seas was in the past not admitted in international law, except in the cases of prescriptive right and occupation.[49] The new continental-shelf doctrine[50] based on economic necessity and modern technological knowledge has been accepted on the consideration that the law could not stand still and fail to provide a satisfactory basis for the reconciliation of conflicting claims and new demands in changing conditions.[51] As the International Law Commission declared, "legal concepts should not impede this development,"[52] and "interference, even if substantial, with navigation and fishing might, in some cases, be justified,"[53] and indeed necessary. Thus this impulse to adapt the law to fresh needs and conditions has been strongly endorsed despite its inevitable obstruction or impairment of the traditionally sacrosanct freedom of the seas, not only in the process of exploitation but also in safeguarding such installations (Texas towers, etc.) as may be established.[54]

Yet another problem of the continental-shelf doctrine is the status of the superjacent waters of the shelf. This involves another major economic interest—fisheries. The earliest appearance of the continental-shelf doctrine, in fact, took the form of claims to monopoly in the name of fishery conservation. This was done by the smaller fishing nations who were responding to the control of major fisheries by the advanced maritime powers, a control maintained with the help of the concept of the freedom of the high seas.[55]

As early as 1910 Portugal maintained that the continental shelf was the birthplace and nursery of young fish, and set forth a regulation to prohibit trawling by steam vessels within the limits of the shelf at the 100-fathom isobath.[56] By 1937 even the United States under the alleged

49. See the cases of sedentary fisheries in Higgins and Colombos, *Law of the Sea*, 1954, p. 58.
50. The I.L.C. adopted the following definition: "The sea bed and subsoil of the submarine areas adjacent to the ocean but outside the area of the territorial sea, to a depth of 200 metres . . . or, beyond that limit, to where the depth of the superjacent waters admits of the exploitation of the natural resources"—Art. 17 of the draft of 1956, in *A.J.I.L.*, LI (1957), supp. 243.
51. See O'Connell, "Sedentary Fisheries," pp. 195-96; see also *Report of I.L.C.*, 5th Sess., p. 22.
52. Cited in "United Nations, Report of I.L.C., Second Session," p. 148; see Gidel, *Plateau continental*, pp. 4, 13-16.
53. Cited in "United Nations, Report of I.L.C., Eighth Session," Off. Doc. 250.
54. The "safety zone" with the recommended "maximum radius of 500 metres" as "sufficient for the purpose" of exploration and supervision may still add to the problem of interference; see *Report of I.L.C.*, 11th Sess., p. 22.
55. Cosford, "Continental Shelf," p. 246; for a good analysis see Garcia Amador, *Resources of the Sea*, p. 70.
56. As cited in *U.N.L.S.*, *High Seas*, 1951, pp. 19-21.

13

threat of a "Japanese invasion" was about to preserve the Alaskan salmon supply by invoking the continental shelf doctrine.[57] This history of close relationship between the continental-shelf idea and the fishery problem makes it understandable that the Presidential Proclamation on Coastal Fisheries should be issued on the very same day as the Proclamation on the Continental Shelf.[58] Citing "an urgent need to protect coastal fishery resources from destructive exploitation," and purporting to give "due regard to conditions peculiar to each region and situation and to the special rights and equities for the coastal state," the Fisheries Proclamation set forth two principles of conservation: a unilateral one and one by agreement with other nations in the region. It disclaimed any intention of affecting the status of the high seas.

This dissociation of the fishery conservation plan from the continental-shelf doctrine was, it seems, specifically intended to discourage other states, particularly Latin American nations, from claiming vast superjacent waters and fishing grounds in conjunction with the continental shelf.[59] For Latin America had a long tradition of political and legal agitation in favor of achieving exclusive fishery rights by extending sovereignty over the high seas. This agitation had grown up against a background of monopolistic control of fisheries by the technologically advanced powers, in particular the United States.[60] In taking this stand, the Latin American nations could argue that they were merely implementing the Truman Proclamation's proviso that "due regard" be given to local conditions and to the "special rights and equities" of coastal states. It was by no accidental decision, then, that the countries of Latin America, disregarding the American distinction between fishery conservation and the continental shelf, were the first to claim such rights of sovereignty over both the continental shelf and its superjacent waters for exclusive fishery conservation.[61]

As one authority recently observed, "there are increasingly strong arguments for the recognition by international law of the establishment of a contiguous zone for fisheries."[62] Most of the small coastal states, joined more recently by the emerging nations, have come to regard the principle of the freedom of the seas as a "sort of colonialism of the

57. See the Copeland Bill (1938) and the Dimond Bill (1937), as cited by Barnes and Gregory, "Alaskan Salmons"; see also Jessup, "Pacific Coast Fisheries," pp. 129-30.

58. 59 Stat. 885 (Presidential Proclamation No. 2668, September 28, 1945).

59. Bingham, "Juridical Status," pp. 5-6; Mouton, *Continental Shelf*, pp. 217-18.

60. Leonard, *International Regulations*, pp. 151, 162-63.

61. Cosford, "Continental Shelf," p. 248.

62. U.N. Gen. Ass., *Memorandum on the Regime of the High Seas by G. Gidel*, p. 36; see Appendix II, below, for the practice of fishing zones.

14

high seas,"[63] and as "outmoded rules of international law which were based on the custom and usage of one or two states only."[64] Thus, in a sort of "cartographic chauvinism,"[65] they have precipitated a fundamental change in the freedom of the seas, either by creating an exclusive fishery zone contiguous to the territorial sea or by erecting a zone of "preferential rights" to protect their "special rights and equities." The most outspoken claim in this respect was made in the Declaration of Santiago on August 18, 1952, by which the governments of Chile, Ecuador, and Peru established a regional 200-mile "Maritime Zone."[66]

This trend, however reasonable, has constituted a profound challenge to the well-established principle that the right to fish on the high seas is no less important than the right to free navigation within the meaning of the freedom of the seas concept.[67]

It is apparent from the above that, despite the general agreement on the principles of freedom of the high seas and of the territorial sea, their mutual relationship has been in a very fluid and uncertain condition. The fluidity of the relationship has been markedly increased by the trend toward extended seaward jurisdiction which has been manifested not only in outright extension of the breadth of the territorial sea, but also by the contiguous-zone and continental-shelf doctrines and the urge to establish exclusive fishery zones. In brief, it may be said that most of the traditional concepts of the international law of the sea, including the vital question of the line of demarcation between the high seas and the territorial sea, have come increasingly to be challenged and modified under the impact of changed economic and political conditions.[68]

DELIMITATION OF THE TERRITORIAL SEA

The question as to how the breadth of the territorial sea should be determined and drawn is basic to the law of the territorial sea. For even if the breadth is agreed upon, different results could be obtained, de-

63. From a statement by Ulloa Stomayor, Peruvian delegate at the U.N. Conference on the Law of the Sea at Geneva in 1958, *Official Records*, III, 6, 7.
64. *Ibid.*, p. 3, statement by Ahmed Shukairi, Saudi Arabian delegate.
65. Boggs, "Seaward Areas," p. 241.
66. Bayitch, *Interamerican Law*, pp. 42-47. In a subsequent incident the *Olympic Challenger* was seized about 100 miles off the coast of Ecuador in 1954, see Sorensen, "Law of the Sea," p. 214; more recently 2 American tuna boats were seized by Ecuador within its maritime zone, see *New York Times*, May 29, 30, 31, June 1, 2, 5, 6, 11, 15, 1963.
67. Sorensen, "Law of the Sea," p. 211; for an extensive analysis see Garcia Amador, *Resources of the Sea*, pp. 68-69, 82-85.
68. Svarlien considers that this new trend may be "of material influence in the future determination of needed international legal norms" concerning the conservation of maritime resources—"Territorial Sea," p. 339.

15

pending upon what is chosen as the point or line from which the breadth is measured. The fundamental difficulties in determining the rules of delimitation stem from the diverse geographical configurations of the coastal lines and the great variety of extent and types of competing interests based on geographical location of the several territorial seas.[69]

Delimitation of the Territorial Sea in General.—The general practice of coastal states has been to measure the extent of the territorial sea from the low-water mark on the shore.[70] But there are two methods by which the outer limit of the sea could be determined from the low-water mark. The first is the *tracé parallèle*: the line of the exterior limit is drawn parallel to the lower-water mark, following exactly the sinuosities thereof.[71] The second is called "the envelope of arcs of circles" (*courbe tangente*): An arc of a circle whose radius is the extent of the territorial sea is drawn from every designated point on the low-water mark, thus creating an envelope of arcs.[72] The most controversial practice of delimitation has been the "straight baseline": The baselines from which the outer limit of the territorial sea is measured are a series of imaginary straight lines drawn between appropriate salient points on the coast.

At the Hague Conference of 1930 only Latvia, Poland, Norway, and Sweden advocated this straight-baseline concept. Describing its coastal configuration containing innumerable islands, islets, and rocks as the *skjaergaard* ("coastal archipelago"), Norway argued that the starting point for calculating the outer limit of the territorial sea was "a line drawn along the 'skjaergaard' between the furthest rocks" and, where there is no *skjaergaard*, between the "extreme points" on the land. Norway concluded that "there is no rule in Norway, regarding the maximum distance between the starting-points of the base line," but various factors—historical, economic, social, and geographical—must be taken into consideration in deciding the distance.[73] This flexible concept of delimitation was upheld in the Grisbadarna Case (*Sweden v. Norway*) in 1909 by the Permanent Court of Arbitration. In measuring the limit of the territorial sea of the island in dispute, the Court declared that it might not be wise to follow all the minor sinuosities of the coast. The reasonable position was held to be that "the delimitation should be made

69. Boggs, "Territorial Sea," p. 542.
70. Point IV of the Hague Conference of 1930, in "League of Nations," *A.J.I.L.*, Supp. 30-31.
71. See League of Nations, *Bases of Discussion*, pp. 35-38.
72. Proposed by the U.S. delegation at the Hague Conference of 1930, see Boggs, *International Boundaries*, p. 189.
73. League of Nations, *Bases of Discussion*, pp. 37-38.

today by tracing a line perpendicularly to the general direction of the coast."[74] In short, it was virtually recognized that the coastal state itself could decide how the general direction of the coast would be drawn by the method of straight baselines.

The Preparatory Commission for the Hague Conference of 1930, pointing out the difficulties with regard "to the choice of the salient points and the distance determining the base line between these points" and to the lack of uniformity, reported that the low-water mark concept was the "only one which can be adopted."[75] Yet many authorities consider that the low-water measurement along all the sinuosities of the coast is "a generally, but not universally, practiced rule."[76] This problem of delimitation could be therefore regarded as one of defining "a law which is in process of formation."[77]

The existence of islands, islets, and reefs in the vicinity of the coastal line creates a further complication. As shown in the practice of states at the Hague Conference, there have not been any agreements as to the following: whether an island in order to have its own territorial sea must lie above water at high tide or at low tide;[78] what the distance between the mainland and islands and between islands should be in order to have a continuous baseline[79]; whether there are different rules on a "coastal archipelago" and an "oceanic archipelago."[80]

The position taken by each coastal state on the method of determining the territorial sea has been largely conditioned by considerations of national interest, geographical location, and actual configuration of the

74. Scott, *Hague Court Reports*, p. 129; see also pp. 110-40.
75. League of Nations, *Bases of Discussion*, p. 38.
76. Higgins and Colombos, *Law of the Sea*, 1945, pp. 74-75; Gidel, *Droit international*, III, 45-152; Smith, *Law and Custom*, pp. 7-9.
77. From the opinion of Walther M. A. Schucking, in League of Nations, *Report of Sub-Committee II*, p. 15.
78. League of Nations, *Bases of Discussion*, p. 54; only Great Britain and her Dominion nations supported the high-tide concept; the U.S., Japan, Germany, Denmark, and the Netherlands supported low-tide elevations; Finland, Norway, and Sweden supported the use of any piece of land "not constantly submerged."
79. *Ibid.*, pp. 48-49; Japan, Great Britain, Rumania, and the U.S. opposed single contiguous belts "irrespective of whether or not they overlap the territorial waters"; Germany and the Netherlands proposed a single belt if "not more than six nautical miles" from the shore; Norway denied that proximity was a basic question.
80. *Ibid.*, pp. 50-51; Great Britain and her Dominion nations rejected the idea that an archipelago, independent or coastal, should be considered a single unit; others held that a single belt could be drawn around an archipelago, provided that its islands were not farther apart than a certain maximum limit: 6 miles for Germany, less than 10 miles for Japan, "double the width" of the territorial sea for the U.S., 12 miles for Latvia; Norway, Finland, and Sweden did not propose a maximum.

coastline. The result has been to leave the whole problem of delimitation in a state of uncertainty.

Delimitation of Bays.—Bays were traditionally considered exceptions to the general principles of delimitation of the territorial sea, mainly because of geographical facts and practical necessity.[81] As pointed out in the North Atlantic Coast Fisheries Arbitration in 1910, "conditions of national and territorial integrity, of defense, of commerce and of industry are all vitally concerned with the control of the bays penetrating the national coast line."[82] Because of the geographical fact that there are innumerable indentations along the coasts of the world, to which different degrees of interests and importance are attached, there has not been any successful attempt to set up a rule to determine what waters have characteristics of a bay.[83]

There has, however, never been any serious doubt that straight baselines may be drawn between the headlands of certain bays and inlets. The Permanent Court of Arbitration in the North Atlantic Coast Fisheries Arbitration, observing that "the three-mile rule is not applied to bays strictly and systematically," said: "The limits of exclusion shall be drawn three miles from a straight line across the bay in the part nearest the entrance at the first point where the width does not exceed ten miles."[84] Yet there is a great diversity in the practices of states as to the extent of straight baselines between the headlands of bays, although as one authority points out, this headland theory could still be "the embryo from which the future rule of international law will probably develop."[85]

The problems of delimiting bays are complicated further by a distinct tendency among states to assert "historic titles" to various large bays or other waters.[86] A specific problem in this respect is the lack of agreement on the definition of historic bays or waters, or rather a disagreement as to what criteria make such assertions legitimate. Traditionally, long usage was considered the sole root of historic or prescriptive title, whether the term "usage" be identified with "continuous and immemorial usage"[87] or with usage "long established and universally un-

81. Smith, *Law and Custom*, pp. 12-14.
82. U.S. North Atlantic Coast Fisheries Arbitration, *Proceedings before the Permanent Court of Arbitration at the Hague*, I, 94.
83. Boggs, "Territorial Sea," p. 549.   84. Scott, *Hague Court Reports*, p. 188.
85. Jessup, *Law of Territorial Waters*, pp. 359, 382; see also Briggs, *Law of Nations*, p. 289; Gidel, *Droit international*, III, 162.
86. Balch, "Hudson Bay," p. 459; the Delaware and Chesapeake are examples of historic bays.
87. See the replies of governments in League of Nations, *Bases of Discussion*, p. 45; Bustamante y Sirvén, *Territorial Sea*, pp. 142-43.

contested."[88] Recent developments, however, seem to indicate another trend: the vital interests or special rights of the coastal state may form a possible basis for rights to a historic bay or waters. Since American states lacked histories sufficiently long to justify the "continuous and immemorial usage" claim, a different justification was found. In 1922 Captain S. R. Storni argued that "the requirements of self-defense or neutrality or . . . [of] ensuring the various navigation and coastal maritime police services"[89] provided a basis for historic title to bays. The Portuguese delegation at the Hague Conference of 1930 raised an interesting question in this regard: "If we respect age-long and immemorial usage which is the outcome of needs experienced by States in long past times, why should we not respect the needs which modern life, with all its improvements and its demands, impose upon States?"[90] Significantly, the Central American Court of Justice in *El Salvador* v. *Nicaragua* in 1917 unanimously declared the Gulf of Fonseca as a "historic bay possessed of the characteristics of a closed sea," defending its decision "from the three-fold point of view of history, geography and the vital interests of the surrounding States."[91]

From this new trend, it becomes doubtful, indeed, whether the term "historic bays" is an appropriate one. Probably the term "vital bays" may prove more distinctive. "This expression," states Gilbert Gidel, "which is placed on a footing of equality with the expression 'historic bay,' sums up in one word the conditions of substance to be fulfilled by the areas in question, whereas the expression 'historic bays' suggested conditions of form only."[92] One is forced to conclude that for historic bays each case still must be determined on its own merits, by weighing the varied interests involved.[93]

88. League of Nations, *Acts of the Conference*, p. 103; Gidel, *Droit international*, III, 651.
89. International Law Association, *Report of the 35th Conference*, 1922, pp. 98, 99.
90. League of Nations, *Acts of the Conference*, p. 106.
91. As cited in *A.J.I.L.*, II (1917), 700; these factors were further explained: "The special geographical configuration that safeguards so many interests of vital importance to the economic, commercial, agricultural and industrial life of the riparian States and the absolute, indispensable necessity required by those primordial interests and the interests of national defense" (p. 705).
92. *Droit international*, III, 629, 635; see also Bourquin, *Baies historiques*, p. 51; McDougal and Burke, *Public Order*, pp. 358-59.
93. Jessup, *Law of Territorial Waters*, p. 362.

3. THE ANGLO-NORWEGIAN
FISHERIES CASE OF 1951

In the eyes of the great maritime powers, the law of the territorial sea has been long considered established. As previously observed, however, most of the concepts of the territorial sea—the three-mile limit for the breadth of the sea, the ten-mile width for bays and islands, and the methods of the delimitation of the sea—have not been settled as general rules of international law. In many respects, these concepts have been agreed upon only in particular treaties and conventions, and have not reached the stage of general practice. The law of the territorial sea has been, therefore, "one of the most unsatisfactory portions of international law."[1]

These perennial questions have been augmented by new problems arising from the scientific, social, economic, and political upheavals or revolutions which have rapidly transformed the traditional views and even the problems of international law. These developments led to expanded activities in the coastal seas and, as a result, to a demand on the part of coastal states for extension of their seaward jurisdiction. The desire to exploit natural resources in submarine areas, to conserve or monopolize fishery grounds, to extend national jurisdiction into the high seas contiguous to the territorial sea—such motives have created a challenge to the hitherto static concepts of the law of the seas and, in particular, the doctrines describing the relationship between the high seas and the territorial sea.

Another dynamic element in the transformation of the law has been the expansion of the system of international law. From the law of the small homogeneous family of nations in Europe among whom it originated, it became that which now claims the allegiance of nations which had no part in building it up. Changes in the sociological structure of the society of nations are increasingly accompanied by alterations in law.[2] The range of legal systems and ideological differences is much wider than in the past, and there have also been far-reaching changes in the comparative influence of units within the international community.[3] In the field of the law of the territorial sea, there appears to be a general rebellion among the small coastal states and emerging nations

1. Riesenfeld, *Protection of Fisheries*, p. ix.
2. Röling, *International Law*, p. xv.
3. Jenks, *Common Law of Mankind*, pp. 2, 65; see also Kuntz, "Changing Law of Nations," p. 78.

against the hitherto great maritime powers and their traditional exclusive influence in molding the law.[4]

It was at this juncture in the development of international law that
the fisheries dispute between Great Britain and Norway was referred to
the attention of the International Court of Justice. There could not be
any doubt that the Court's judgment would inevitably reflect the uncertain background of the law of the sea and the forces of change, in its
examination of the law in mid-twentieth-century perspective, and would
thus transcend the merely technical and particular points in the dispute.[5]
The membership of the International Court itself was indicative of this
trend, consisting of judges of various nationalities representing "the
main forms of civilization and . . . the principal legal system of the
world."[6]

THE PRINCIPAL ISSUES

The case began with the application of the British government on
September 28, 1949. Norway accepted the compulsory jurisdiction of
the Court in accordance with Article 36, paragraph 2, of the Statute of
the International Court of Justice. Although the litigation formally concerned an exclusive "fisheries zone," it was recognized by the parties
and by the Court that what was actually involved was the territorial sea
of Norway.[7] Both parties having agreed that the territorial sea was in
this case four miles in its extent,[8] the only issue before the Court was
the validity of the Norwegian method of delimiting such a sea.

The dispute involved the provisions of the Norwegian Royal Decree
of July 12, 1935, which delimited the territorial sea along the northern
coast of Norway. The decree was allegedly founded "on the basis of
well-established national titles of rights; by reason of the geographical
conditions prevailing on the Norwegian coasts; in safeguard of the vital
interests of the inhabitants of the northernmost parts of the country."[9]

4. See U.N. Conference on the Law of the Seas, *Official Records*, III, 3, 4, 6,
7, for statements by delegations of small nations refuting the 3-mile limit for the
territorial sea and also the traditional concept of the freedom of the seas.
5. Smith, "Fisheries Case," p. 283; also Lauterpacht, "Freedom of the Seas."
6. Art. 9 of the Statute of the I.C.J.; see also Art. 38, paragraph 1, which enu-
merates a source of international law as "the general principle of law recognized
by civilized nations"; see note 14, below, for the nationalities of the judges.
7. I.C.J., *Reports*, p. 125; see also I.C.J., *Pleadings*, I, 18.
8. The admission of the 4-mile limit by the British government was of the
greatest significance to Norway, as Jens Evensen comments, "especially because
of the vigorous British protestations for the long period of time that Norway had
no such rights"—"Fisheries Case," p. 611.
9. I.C.J., *Pleadings*, I, 14-15.

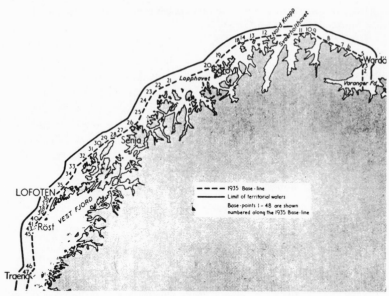

Fig. 1.—THE DELIMITATION BY THE NORWEGIAN ROYAL DECREE OF 1935
Source: Waldock, "The Anglo-Norwegian Fisheries Case," *British Yearbook of International Law*, XXVIII (1951), 115.

In the decree 47 straight baselines at 48 base points were drawn all along the area in dispute, varying in length according to the geographical conditions.[10] (See Figure 1.) According to this "Norwegian," or baseline, system, straight baselines were drawn between the headlands of bays and all the Norwegian fjords on the mainland and, when there were islands, islets, or reefs off the mainland, between the most extreme of such islands, islets, and reefs. The four-mile extent of the territorial sea was then measured from these straight baselines.

Great Britain maintained first that international law does not give each state a right to choose arbitrarily the baselines for its territorial sea. The fundamental rule was that the territorial sea of a state must be measured from the actual coastlines by the method of the "envelope of the arcs of circles" (*courbe tangente*). (See Figure 2.) Great Britain permitted only "historic titles" to "certain fjords and sounds" of the area in dispute, which fall within the definition of bays as "exceptions to the main rule, strictly limited by international law." In the view of Great Britain, therefore, straight baselines were permitted only across

10. The longest baseline was 40 miles across the Vestfjord, those across Svaerholthavet and Varangerfjord being 38.6 and 30 miles, respectively; 20 more lines varied between 26.5 and 11.7 miles—*ibid.*, pp. 86-87, 199-204.

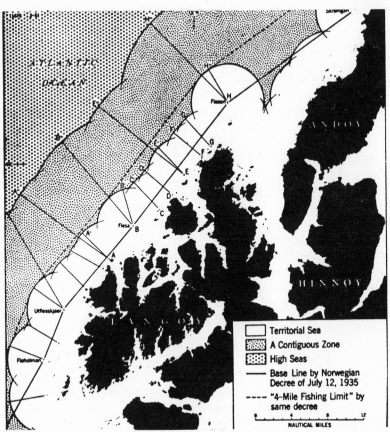

Fig. 2.—SEAWARD LIMIT OF THE TERRITORIAL SEA. On a portion of the northwest coast of Norway the technique of laying down the outer limit of the territorial sea is here illustrated. The Norwegian claim of a four-mile limit is used. Note the difference between the straight baseline system (base points, A, B, H, etc.; the outer limit, the dotted line) and the "envelope of the arcs of circles of four-mile radius drawn from all points on the coast" (A, B, C, D, E, etc.); the former method was used by the Norwegian Royal Decree of 1935, while the latter method was suggested by Great Britain. For purposes of illustration a contiguous zone twelve miles wide is here assumed, constituting the arcs of A", B", E", H", etc.

Source: Boggs, "Delimitation of Seaward Areas under National Jurisdiction," American Journal of International Law, XLV (1951), 259.

the openings of bays. A bay was defined as "a well-marked indentation, whose penetration inland is in such proportion to the width of its mouth as to constitute more than a mere curvature of the coast." The base-lines, in any case, could not exceed ten miles in length.[11]

11. I.C.J., Reports, pp. 121, 122; see also I.C.J., Pleadings, I, 57, 70.

23

Norway, on the other hand, argued that there was no general hard and fast rule in international law concerning delimitation which would prescribe a ten-mile limit across the mouth of a bay and also a three-, four-, six-, or twelve-mile limit for the territorial belt.[12] Rejecting the British contention of a historic title to exception, the Norwegian counsel stated that "the Norwegian Government does not rely upon history to justify exceptional rights, to claim an area of sea which general law would deny," but "it invokes history, together with other factors, to justify the way in which it applies the general law."[13] To Norway, therefore, her method of delimitation, following "the general direction of the coast," was an application of the general rule. It is of interest to note that Norway was not willing to accept its delimitation as "exceptional" from the British concept of general rules of international law, thus challenging the traditionally held Anglo-American concept of historical exception.

The Court was thus brought to examine the fundamental philosophy behind the diametrically opposed viewpoints of the two parties as to the nature and problems of the territorial sea in general.

THE DECISION, WITH CONCURRING AND DISSENTING OPINIONS

The International Court of Justice, after deliberating six weeks, delivered a surprisingly short judgment of twenty-seven pages. The Court found, by 10 votes to 2[14], that the method employed in the delimitation of the fisheries zone by the Norwegian Royal Decree of July 12, 1935, was "not contrary to international law," and found, by 8 to 4,[15] that the actual baselines fixed by the said decree in application of this method were "not contrary to international law."

The Court began its judgment by observing the peculiar geographic realities of Norway and declared that "What matters, what really constitutes the Norwegian coast line, is the outer line of 'skjaergaard.'" On the problem of delimitation, the Court found both the *tracé parallèle*

12. I.C.J., *Reports*, pp. 396, 412, 444-48; I.C.J., *Pleadings*, III, 239, 242, 245, 253-62.

13. I.C.J., *Pleadings*, I, 574.

14. Of the Court's 15 judges, 12 participated in the case: J. G. Guerrero (El Salvador), J. Basdevant (France), A. Alvarez (Chile), G. H. Hackworth (U.S.), B. Winiarski (Poland), M. Zoricic (Yugoslavia), C. de Visscher (Belgium), H. Klaestad (Norway), A. H. Badawi (Egypt), Hsu Mo (China), A. McNair (Great Britain), and J. E. Read (Canada); I. Fabela Alfaro (Mexico) and S. Krylov (Soviet Union) were absent; I. Azevedo (Brazil) had recently died. Only McNair and Read dissented.

15. Negative votes were cast by McNair, Read, Hsu Mo, and another judge whose name is not given.

and the *courbe tangente* "not obligatory by law," and set forth as an inclusive general rule of delimitation that "the belt of territorial waters must follow the general direction of the coast." In applying this principle to a particular coast line, the Court asserted that the coastal state should take into consideration the following criteria: "the close dependence of the territorial sea upon the land domain," the selected baselines "to be sufficiently closely linked to the land domain," and "certain economic interests peculiar to a region, the reality and importance of which are clearly evidenced by a long usage." Finally, the Court considered historic factors, such as long practice and usage and acquiescence by other states, also significant in conjunction with the above criteria for the justification of the Norwegian system of delimitation. In this respect, however, the Court stated that "too much importance need not be attached to the few uncertainties or contradictions, real or apparent." Furthermore, in considering a contested baseline across the Lopphavet basin, the Court declared that the rule of the general direction of the coast is "devoid of any mathematical precision" and the selected baseline was kept "within the bounds of what is moderate and reasonable." Because of these and other geographic and economic factors, the Court found that the Norwegian system of fixing the baselines across bays and even mere curvatures, and between islands, islets, and drying rocks, is "the application of general international law to a specific case."[16]

The Court also reiterated the well-established principle that "it is the land which confers upon the coastal State a right to the waters off its coast" and "the delimitation of sea areas has always an international aspect; it cannot be dependent merely upon the will of the coastal State."[17] On the other hand, the Court clearly rejected as established general rules of international law the ten-mile rule for bays, the *tracé parallèle* and *courbe tangente*, and the strict application of historic exceptions.

This greater flexibility in delimitation the Court's judgment pointed to was accentuated by Judge Alvarez in his concurring opinion. Pointing out the inadequacy of the Anglo-Saxon concept of law in the changing world, Alvarez asserted that the new international law is "not exclusively juridical," that "it has also aspects which are political, economic, social, psychological, etc." Then in a sweeping statement, he stated that "having regard to the great variety of the geographical and economic conditions of States, it is not possible to lay down uniform rules, applicable to all, governing the extent of the territorial sea and the way in

16. I.C.J., *Reports*, pp. 127-42.
17. I.C.J., *Reports*, p. 133.

which it is to be reckoned." In fixing the breadth of the territorial sea and its delimitation, according to Alvarez, all a state must do is to "indicate the reasons, geographic, economic, etc., which provide the justification therefor."[18]

The judges of the traditional school of international law were not in agreement even among themselves. Judge Hackworth concurred only "in the operative part of the Judgment" for "the Norwegian Government has proved the existence of an historic title to the disputed area of waters." Judge Hsu Mo also accepted the operative part of the Norwegian system upon the proof of historic exception. He stated that the Norwegian system is "not so much the direct application of the general rule as the degree of deviation from the general rule that is to be considered." But he disagreed with the Court on the two baselines drawn across Svaerholthavet and Lopphavet, asserting that Norway had "not succeeded in establishing any historic titles to the waters in question."[19] Finally, McNair and Read dissented. They pointed out the lack of historic titles for Norway to claim exception from the coastline rule and the ten-mile rule for bays, and asserted that a series of imaginary straight lines should not be "drawn by the coastal State for the purpose of giving effect, *even within reasonable limits*, to its economic and other social interests and to other subjective factors."[20]

To sum up: The Anglo-Norwegian Fisheries Case became an historic case by the simple fact that it was adjudicated during the crucial stage of transformation of the law of the sea and managed to involve the various basic issues of the law, including its philosophy. The International Court, delivering such a short decision with a clear majority in favor of Norway, categorically defeated the British contentions, which had been long considered authoritative because of the predominant role Great Britain had played in molding the law of the sea. In this respect, the Court, having set forth inclusive principles of the law and flexible criteria valid for any delimitation, was clear not only in denying the hard and fast rules of traditional international law, but also in upholding the flexibility and adaptability of the general principles of the law and supporting the modern trend toward transformation of the law itself. This is true particularly when the majority opinion, inundated by the sweeping phrases of Alvarez, is considered in reference to the dissenting opinions of McNair and Read who, supported in principle by Hsu Mo and Hackworth, championed in vain the traditional view.

18. I.C.J., *Reports*, pp. 146, 149, 150.   19. I.C.J., *Reports*, pp. 144, 155, 157.
20. I.C.J., *Reports*, pp. 161, 183, 187, 192, 201 (italics added); see also pp. 158, 160.

LEGAL ANALYSIS OF THE DECISION

The Rule of the General Direction of the Coast.—In refuting the ten-mile rule for bays and islands and the coastline rule as the established rules of international law, the Court introduced as a general principle that "the belt of territorial waters must follow the general direction of the coast" which "makes it possible to fix certain criteria valid for any delimitation of the territorial sea."[21] According to this principle, it appears immaterial whether the belt of the territorial sea is measured from straight baselines, which the Court justified in the Norwegian case, or from the line of the low-water mark along the entire coast according to the *courbe tangente* (the arcs of circles method), or indeed, the *tracé parallèle*.[22] For the Court did not assert that the arcs of circles and the *tracé parallèle* were illegal; it merely held that these methods were not binding on, nor obligatory for, Norway within the principle of the general direction of the coast.[23]

The underlying rationale of this principle, and indeed of the whole law relating to the territorial sea, the Court intimated, is that "the delimitation of sea areas has always an international aspect; it cannot be dependent merely upon the will of the coastal State as expressed in municipal law."[24] But the elastic criteria which the Court established for testing the "international aspect" of any delimitation would seem to defeat the purpose of this basic doctrine. For the Court did not accept the basic British contention, the traditional principle that recognition or acquiescence of other states alone permit any valid exception or prescriptive title in any delimitation. Hence, "this rather half-hearted attempt to save the ultimate authority of international law," states one authority, "affords a fragile safeguard against the dangers implicit in the essentially subjective character of the new test which may well serve as an invitation to states to put forward extravagant claims to appropriate areas of the open sea."[25]

The actual criteria of the principle of the general direction of the coast, by which the validity under international law of any given delimitation will be tested, tend indeed to be subjective and "liberal."[26]

21. I.C.J., *Reports*, p. 129.
22. See Lauterpacht, *Development of International Law*, pp. 191-92, for his criticism that the Court elevated a minority practice—the straight-baseline method—to an accepted rule of international law.
23. See Johnson, "Fisheries Case," pp. 157-58; Waldock, "Fisheries Case," pp. 152-53.   24. I.C.J., *Reports*, p. 133.   25. Brierly, *Law of Nations*, p. 176.
26. The term "liberal" is used in this work to mean "not rigidly bound by established concepts," or "free from hard and fast rules within the bounds of reason."

The first criterion is "the close dependence of the territorial sea upon the land domain" because "it is the land which confers upon the coastal State a right to the waters off its coasts." When this criterion is satisfied, the Court declares, the coastal state should be allowed "the latitude necessary in order to be able to adapt its delimitation to practical needs and local requirements."[27]

√ The second criterion is "the more or less close relationship existing between certain sea areas and the land formations which divide or surround them" or the question of whether the sea areas lying within the baselines are "sufficiently closely linked to the land domain to be subject to the regime of internal waters."

The third criterion, "beyond purely geographical factors," is the consideration of "certain economic interests peculiar to a region, the reality and importance of which are clearly evidenced by a long usage."[28] The Court, after viewing the "geographical realities" of Norway, describing them as "these barren regions" where "the inhabitants of the coastal zone derive their livelihood essentially from fishing," maintained that these criteria should be liberally applied. And indeed the Court had stated that the general direction of the coast is "devoid of any mathematical precision." Because of these geographical and economic criteria the Court concluded that the Norwegian system was not so much an exceptional system as "the application of general international law to a specific case," and "an adaptation rendered necessary by local conditions."[29]

√ Finally, the Court included historic factors, long usage, and acquiescence by other states. It is of utmost significance, however, to note that the Court did not really consider historic title as such to be a criterion. In its pleadings, Norway had advanced the contention that the Court should consider not only the vital economic interest in fishing resources but also geographical, topographical, and hydrographical factors in deciding the amount of discretion to be allowed a coastal state in the scope and method of its delimitation.[30] The fundamental position of Great Britain, on the other hand, was that, "except in certain exceptional cases" evidenced singularly by historic titles, the belt of the territorial sea must

27. The criteria are set forth in I.C.J., *Reports*, p. 133; see also Alvarez' consideration of the necessary factors for any delimitation, p. 150.
28. See also the later reference to the Norwegian "rights, founded on the vital needs of the population and attested by very ancient and peaceful usage"—I.C.J., *Reports*, p. 142.
29. I.C.J., *Reports*, pp. 128, 131, 133, 142.
30. Rejoinder by Norway, presented by Sven Arntzen, I.C.J., *Pleadings*, III, 11, 12-13; Oral Pleadings by Maurice Bourquin, IV, 175-77, 179; Counter-Memorial by Arntzen, I, 372-73.

28

be "measured from low-water mark on the land as the base-line whether the land be the mainland or islands." Therefore, it is quite irrelevant for the measurement of territorial waters "whether the best fishing grounds are inside or outside the dividing line; whether the population of the State concerned are fishermen depending on fishing."[31] Sir Eric Beckett in defense of the British position argued against the Norwegian system: "So supple and flexible is it that you cannot seize it at any point without it changing its form. It takes into account so many local considerations of which the Norwegian Government is the judge."[32]

As Hackworth and Hsu Mo observed, the Norwegian system could have been justified by prescriptive or historic title alone. But the Court rendered its approval of the Norwegian contention that it did "not rely upon history to justify exceptional rights, to claim areas of sea which the general law denies," but rather it invoked "history, together with other factors, to justify the way in which it applies the general law."[33] This obviously demonstrates that the historic factor was really considered a complementary element rather than a strict and singularly inflexible factor.

The criteria used to establish the legitimacy of the Norwegian claims are so flexible that, one authority asserts, the validity of any claim appears "a matter of guess-work."[34] In the case of the Lopphavet, a line 62 miles long passing to seaward of an island-dotted area and merely touching one submerging rocklet on the way, was described by the Court as having been "kept within the bounds of what is moderate and reasonable," even though the Lopphavet basin "constitutes an ill-defined geographical whole." Moreover, the Court asserted that the general direction of the coast is "devoid of any mathematical precision," and one should neither "confine oneself to examine one sector of the coast alone" nor "rely on the impression that may be gathered from a large-scale chart of this sector alone." The use of small-scale charts recommended here tends to magnify the peculiarity of the coastal line and to invite different interpretations of the general direction of the coast rule itself.[35] In the case of the Svaerholthavet, where "several lines can be envisaged" over seven bays, the Court maintained that Norway "would seem to be in the best position to appraise the local conditions dictating the selection," and a line 38.6 miles long, enclosing all the bays at once,

31. Statement by Sir Frank Soskice, I.C.J., *Pleadings*, IV, 26, 30.
32. I.C.J., *Pleadings*, IV, 371-72.
33. I.C.J., *Reports*, p. 133.
34. Waldock, "Fisheries Case," p. 149.
35. Hsu Mo was critical of the Court's decision on this point, as giving "a too liberal interpretation so that the coastline is almost completely ignored."

was allowed "in the light of all the geographical factors involved," even though some doubt was cast on historic factors.[36]

Within the terms of the above criteria, a coastal state may be encouraged to select baselines which do not follow the physical contour of the coast but consist of a series of imaginary straight lines drawn between arbitrarily designated points on the mainland and off-lying islands and even rocks, without particular regard to their distance.

Bays, Islands, Reefs, and the General Direction of the Coast.—In the initial pleadings, Great Britain invited the Court to define a bay as "a well-marked indentation, whose penetration inland is in such proportion to the width of its mouth as to constitute more than a mere curvature of the coast."[37] It also set forth the ten-mile baseline for bays in general, providing for the exceptional case of an historic bay. On the other hand, Norway denied not only the proposition that there exists any maximum extent for bays in international law but also the purely juridical concept of bays, stating: "Chaque baie a sa physionomie propre, qui est déterminée par des circonstances diverses, d'ordre géographique, historique, politique, économique."[38] These opinions were obviously based on diametrically different philosophies.

The Court in one paragraph struck down the British contention. It held that, despite the various treaties, conventions, and arbitral decisions to the contrary, "the ten-mile rule has not acquired the authority of a general rule of international law."[39] As simple as that! The Court said nothing, furthermore, about a general limit on the width of bays.

The point at issue here was faced by the Court in the Svaerholthavet problem. It was whether the "penetration inland" should be taken to be the tip of the Svaerholt peninsula (11.5 miles inside the baseline drawn by Norway) or the innermost points of the Lakesfjord and the Porsangerfjord. The fjords are separated by the peninsula and penetrate inland, respectively 50 and 75 miles from the baseline. All of these geographical features make it, one authority claims, "all a matter of appreciation, difficult to define precisely whether the Svaerholthavet is one bay or a number of separate bays."[40] The Court, considering the matter in the light of all the geographical factors involved, found that it was one bay. It also asserted that when several lines could be envisaged

36. I.C.J., *Reports*, pp. 131, 141, 142, 144, 154.
37. Memorial by Beckett, I.C.J., *Pleadings*, I, 70; see Waldock, "Fisheries Case," pp. 137-38, for the numerous precedents cited in the British Written Reply.
38. Norwegian Rejoinder by Arntzen, I.C.J., *Pleadings*, III, 319; see also Bourquin, *Baies historiques*, pp. 37-38.
39. I.C.J., *Reports*, p. 131.
40. Johnson, "Fisheries Case," pp. 167-68.

as in this case, "the coastal State would seem to be in the best position to appraise the local conditions dictating the selection." Then the Court went on to destroy the basis of the British contention, maintaining that it could not share the view of Great Britain that Norway was confronted with an exceptional case because of its skjaergaard and fjords: "all that the Court can see therein is the application of general international law to a specific case."[41] The Court without doubt reduced the importance of the conception of a bay in any strict sense by leaving to the coastal state a great deal of discretion in choosing the baselines for delimitation.

At the same time, the Court swept aside any notion of delimiting bays by the geometric calculation traditionally considered significant, when it admitted that the straight baselines could be used "not only in the case of well-defined bays, but also in cases of minor curvatures of the coastline where it was solely a question of giving a simpler form to the belt of territorial waters."[42] All in all, the intention of the Court from the beginning of its judgment seemed to reduce all features of any coastal line to the basic principle of the "general direction of the coast," thus allowing "very little room for any distinct rule for bays." The Court's decision, moreover, made virtually useless the conception of historic bays or waters, which have been long considered as an exception from ordinary bays or waters in the sense that they require "long usage," "prescriptive title," or "immemorial usage." There seems in the Court's opinion hardly "room left for the classical distinction between historic and other bays."[43]

Norway began its pleadings, in the Counter-Memorial by Arntzen, with the contention that "la portée exacte de cette théorie reste à certains égards imprécise," and "la Norvège n'a pas besoin de faire appel à la théorie des eaux historiques pour justifier son système." The contention with regard to historic bays or waters was simply that the time factor must be considered with "other factors," such as "conditions géographiques," "intérêts vitaux," "exigences de la sécurité nationale" and "conditions de la vie économique du pays."[44] Undoubtedly, Norway favored the theory of "vital" bays discussed in Chapter 2.

Great Britain, on the other hand, strictly conforming to the traditional school which based historic title on the acquiescence of other states, asserted that "under the most fundamental norm of international

41. I.C.J., *Reports*, pp. 131, 141; for a comprehensive analysis of this last passage see Nakamura, "Significance of the Fisheries Case," pp. 252, 254-55.

42. I.C.J., *Reports*, pp. 129-30.

43. Waldock, "Fisheries Case," p. 141; a critical analysis to this effect is on pp. 155-56; see also Smith, "Fisheries Case," p. 299.

44. I.C.J., *Pleadings*, I, 564, 572, 574.

law the rules governing the extent of maritime territory are grounded in the consent of States."[45]

The Court, ruling decisively in favor of the Norwegian contention, declared that despite the "paucity of evidence" in Norway's historic claims to certain areas in dispute,[46] "too much importance need not be attached to the few uncertainties or contradictions, real or apparent" in proving "long usage" or "acquiescence."[47] Not only does the Court's heavy reliance on factors such as geography and economics tend to ignore the distance of the straight baselines across bays, but it largely appears to reduce the significance of any proof of historic title. The diminished role which the Court assigned to long usage is especially surprising in view of the comparative recency of the "vital bays" theory. As McNair and Read pointed out in their dissenting opinions, the Norwegian Supreme Court had publicly enunciated this system of delimitation only in 1934, in the *St. Just* decision.[48] In this instance also Alvarez appeared to punctuate the meaning and spirit of the Court's judgment when he asserted that "international law does not lay down any specific duration of time necessary for prescription to take effect" and also that "a comparatively recent usage relating to the territorial sea may be of greater effect than an ancient usage insufficiently proved."[49]

In any case, as one authority notes, "since the Court had already found that the general rules of international law as laid down by the Court, did in themselves justify the Norwegian delimitation, it was *strictly unnecessary* for it to go into the issue of historic rights."[50]

The liberal principle of the general direction of the coast was also applied very flexibly in the case of the Norwegian coastal archipelagos. From the beginning the Court stressed the "geographical realities" which forced it to consider such archipelagos as "a whole with the mainland," asserting "the outer line of the 'skjaergaard'" as the starting point of the territorial delimitation. As a consequence, the Court, flatly rejected the British contention that straight baselines could be drawn only across bays, intimated that "there is no valid reason to draw them only across bays . . . and not also to draw them between islands, islets and rocks, across the sea areas separating them, even when such areas do not fall within the conception of a bay," and concluded that "it is sufficient

45. I.C.J., *Pleadings*, II, 642 (British Reply); see also pp. 398-401.
46. See the comment by Green, "Fisheries Case," p. 376.
47. I.C.J., *Reports*, p. 138; see p. 142 for the Court's observation on the Lopphavet basin.
48. I.C.J., *Reports*, pp. 183, 201.
49. I.C.J., *Reports*, p. 152.
50. Fitzmaurice, "General Principles and Sources," p. 27.

that they should be situated between the island formations of the 'skjaer-gaard,' *inter fauces terrarum.*[51]

The extremely liberal application of waters *inter fauces terrarum* is evidenced in the Court's treatment of the Lopphavet basin, which is an extensive area of waters dotted with large islands and submerged reefs that are separated by inlets terminating in the various fjords. The base-line across this area starts from a rock near the island of Soroy, runs to an isolated submerged rock 44 miles distant, and thence extends a fur-ther 18 miles to another rock 3.5 miles from the island of Kvaloy. A large area within this 62-mile line was regarded by Great Britain as open sea, but was held by the Court on purely geographical factors to be Norwegian inland waters and therefore, presumably, *inter fauces terrarum.*[52]

In reference to the length of straight baselines between islands, the Court declared that "attempts that have been made analogous to the limitations concerning bays (distance between the islands not exceeding twice the breadths of the territorial waters, or 10 or 12 sea miles), have not got beyond the state of proposals."[53] In other words, the joining of straight baselines between units of an archipelago is not subject to any definite limit on the length of the lines.

Another conspicuous aspect of the Court's judgment is its treatment of those waters lying between and inside the coastal archipelagos, that is, inside the straight baselines, as belonging to the internal regime, rather than having the status of a strait. Great Britain had argued that the intervening water route, called "Indreleia," was a part of the terri-torial sea and as such open to the right of innocent passage. The Court held, however, that the Indreleia is not a strait at all, but rather a navigational route prepared as such by means of artificial aids to navi-gation provided by Norway. Thus the water route is closed to the right of innocent passage.[54]

The Seaward Jurisdiction.—Although, as mentioned above, the extent of the territorial sea was not formally involved in this case, there is a

51. I.C.J., *Reports*, pp. 128, 130.
52. I.C.J., *Reports*, p. 141; see Johnson, "Fisheries Case," p. 168, for a critical remark on this as "the weakest part of the entire judgment."
53. I.C.J., *Reports*, p. 131; for an analysis see Vaughan, "Norwegian Fisheries Zone," pp. 303-4.
54. I.C.J., *Reports*, p. 132; British Rejoinder by Beckett, I.C.J., *Pleadings*, I, 79-83. In the case of a coastal archipelago, the Court in 1949 declared that it con-stituted an international strait through which an absolute right of innocent pas-sage even for warships must be guaranteed. The present concept of the Court may conflict with the 1949 decision—see the *Corfu Channel Case*, I.C.J., *Reports, 1949*, pp. 28-29.

close relationship between the problems of delimitation and of the extent of the sea. It is obvious that the width of the territorial sea will vary in dependence on the method of delimitation employed. That is why the fact that the agreement of the parties on the extent of the territorial sea (four-mile limit)[55] is not as significant as it might appear. The agreement is further attenuated by the fact that the ways in which Great Britain and Norway arrived at the four-mile limit were so different in principle that this difference was more significant than the agreement on the number of miles.

The fundamental position of Great Britain was that "a State is entitled to a belt of territorial waters of a certain breadth,"[56] "not optional, not dependent upon the will of the States, but compulsory," under the rule of international law.[57] Only with "a title by long usage" as evidenced in the Norwegian case would a state be entitled to exception.[58] Thus, a consideration of economic and geographical factors, which are by nature subjective and flexible, is "legally completely irrelevant to the issue";[59] "a right to delimit its territorial waters in the manner required to protect its economic and other social interests" is a "novelty"; and "the approbation of such a practice would have a dangerous tendency in that it would encourage States to adopt a subjective appreciation of their rights instead of conforming to a common international standard."[60]

On the other hand, Norway contended that it is the land which confers upon a coastal State the right to its adjacent waters for the protection of its "legitimate interests."[61] Therefore Norway asserted that all the formulae found at one epoch or another in state practices—the range of vision, cannon shot, and modern diverse numerical limits—have simply given concrete expression to the fundamental norm of the coastal state's legitimate interests, inevitably varied as proved at the Hague Codification Conference of 1930.[62] Within this theory of legitimate interest, there could hardly be room for the historic exception,

---

55. I.C.J., *Pleadings*, II, 392-98, 421-23, for the British Reply by Sir Eric Beckett.
56. Oral Pleadings, I.C.J., *Pleadings*, IV, 26.
57. McNair's dissenting opinion, I.C.J., *Reports*, pp. 158, 160.
58. British Memorial by Beckett, I.C.J., *Pleadings*, I, 21; Oral Pleadings by Soskice, IV, 25-26.
59. Statement by Soskice, I.C.J., *Pleadings*, IV, 30; see also p. 377.
60. McNair's dissent, I.C.J., *Reports*, p. 169.
61. Counter-Memorial by Arntzen, I.C.J., *Pleadings*, I, 372-73, 562; see also III, 11, IV, 175-77, 178-79.
62. I.C.J., *Pleadings*, I, 375-76.

which the British applied in their concession to the Norwegian four-mile limit.

In this confrontation of diametrically opposed views, the Court carefully but equivocally delivered its opinion. The Court, maintaining that "the delimitation of sea areas has always an international aspect," argued that "the validity of the delimitation with regard to other States depends upon international law."[63] At first glance, this passage seems to support the British contention. But analysis of the Court's criteria which test the validity of any delimitation and of its international aspect, nevertheless, brings the Court's opinion closer to the Norwegian contention and tends to disqualify the British proposition. Moreover, in its liberal and general spirit,[64] the Court could not but consider "international law" in terms of the rapidly changing law of the middle of the twentieth century, rather than in terms of Grotius and Bynkershoek.[65]

The most complete endorsement of the Norwegian argument was given by Judge Alvarez in his concurring opinion, which has as one authority points out "the merit of formulating a general principle" clearly bringing out the implications of the Court's judgment.[66] In rejecting the purely juridical nature of the law of the territorial sea, Alvarez declared that "with regard to the great variety of the geographical and economic conditions of States, it is not possible to lay down uniform rules." Consequently, "each State may . . . determine the extent of its territorial sea," indicating the reasons—geographic, economic, social, and political—which provide the justification for its legitimacy.[67]

As previously shown, the regime of the territorial sea has become increasingly interwoven with other seaward jurisdictions, such as the contiguous zones and the continental shelf. Consequently, the liberal approach of the Court to the problems of the territorial sea could be considered applicable to these related areas. This implication was clearly indicated by Alvarez, who seemed to be inviting coastal states to expand their seaward jurisdictions. It is not surprising, therefore, that Alvarez approved the contiguous-zone practice and the reserved coastal areas

---

63. I.C.J., *Reports*, p. 132.

64. The Court approached the case with such general terms as "valid for *any* delimitation of the territorial sea," and certain "basic considerations *inherent in the nature* of the territorial sea"—I.C.J., *Reports*, pp. 129, 133; italics added.

65. See to this effect the statements by the Argentine and Tunisian delegations and by F. V. Garcia Amador at the Geneva Conference in 1958, in U.N. Conference on the Law of the Sea, *Official Records*, III, 37, 42, 45; see also Waldock, "Fisheries Case," pp. 130-31, 147-53; cf. Svarlien, "Territorial Sea," p. 343.

66. Johnson, "Fisheries Case," p. 173.

67. I.C.J., *Reports*, p. 150.

for exploitation of the wealth of the continental shelf, individually or regionally contended.[68]

Significance of the Case.—In reference to transformation of the law of the territorial sea, the Court's "daring piece of legislation," as Lauterpacht puts it,[69] was "the first authoritative"[70] and "realistic recognition that economic interests—as well as those of defense, police power and national pride—are important justifications for seaward jurisdiction."[71] In its outright disregard of the historic attitudes of the great maritime powers represented by Great Britain, and with its sanction of the flexible and adaptable nature of the general principle of international law, the Court was apparently sympathetic toward "the modern tendency . . . to whittle down the principles of the freedom of the seas in favour of coastal States."[72] In general, therefore, the Court appears to have lent to the law of the territorial sea "a bias or presumption in favour of the coastal State"[73] against the general interests of the freedom of the seas and other states.

As one authority observes, "the Court's judgment has disposed of several notions which have sometimes been alleged, particularly in Anglo-American practice, to be rules of international law.[74] The Court reduced the significance of such notions as the coastline rule, the ten-mile rule for bays and islands, the prescriptive titles to exceptions, including historic bays and waters, and the rigid and mechanical three-mile rule for the extent of the territorial sea—all are denied as general rules of international law under the criteria for the rule of the general direction of the coast.

By far the most salient aspect of the Court's judgment, however, is found in its obvious awareness of "the function of custom and its necessarily evolutionary character." This is manifested in the Court's overwhelming endorsement of and emphasis on reasonableness and adaptability in applying the general rules of international law to specific cases in diverse economic, political, social, and geographical situations. The customary rules, such as those of the law of the territorial sea, are the

68. *Ibid.*; see Evensen's analysis in "Fisheries Case," p. 626.

69. "Freedom of the Seas."

70. Manley O. Hudson's observation on the case in United Nations, *Yearbook of the International Law Commission*, 1952, I, 172; hereafter this *Yearbook* will be cited as *Yearbook of I.L.C.*

71. "International Court Upholds Norway's Measurement of Territorial Sea," p. 1455.

72. Green, "Fisheries Case," p. 377.

73. Johnson, "Fisheries Case," pp. 170, 175.

74. Young, "Fisheries Case," p. 244; see also Johnson, "Fisheries Case," p. 177; Svarlien, "Territorial Sea," p. 343.

sources of living law only insofar as, by adhering to the flexibility of their own process, they are capable of providing states with an adequate basis which could be adapted to the diverse facts in question.[75] Far from denoting a disintegration of the law, these adaptations, as long as they are inspired by the realities of international practices and trends, are proof of the progress of the law, although in its transitional phase "great doubts exist as to the valid principles of law applicable" to specific cases.[76] The Court without doubt acknowledged in this spirit the nature of modern international law as neither static nor "exclusively juridical" but "dynamic," discovering in it "aspects which are political, economic, social, psychological, etc.," as Alvarez best put it.[77] In so considering, the Court's judgment in this case lent its moral sanction, if not actual vindication, to the existing trend toward transforming the law of the territorial sea, signifying "an important turning point"[78] in the progress of the law, rather than "an innovation in the law."[79]

Moreover, this important decision was reached with the background of several uncertainties in traditional international law which had in the past brought many "older" members of the community of nations into conflicts, and at the time when the rapidly expanding range or scope of the law and the community still did not include many subsequently independent Asian and African nations. Thus the Court's judgment included in itself potential of wider application and interpretation, not only among the dissatisfied members of the community but also among the increasing number of the newly emerging nations.

75. De Visscher, "Reflections on Present Prospects," p. 473.
76. Evensen, "Fisheries Case," p. 149.
77. I.C.J., *Reports*, p. 149.
78. Johnson, "The Fisheries Case," p. 180.
79. Brierly, *Law of Nations*, p. 175.

4. LEGAL ANALYSIS
OF FURTHER DEVELOPMENTS

T he International Court in the Fisheries Case has done more than settle a single dispute. In providing this first authoritative pronouncement for the changing law of the seas, the Court has not so much answered all the problems that may in the future arise in connection with the delimitation of the territorial sea as it has set forth certain guiding principles for the evolution of modern international law. No less important is the Court's attempt to clarify the various uncertainties in the law of the territorial sea as traditionally held among the great maritime powers. For the hard and fast concept of traditional law, the Court has substituted the criteria of reason, moderation, justice, and equity. The Court in effect invited states and international bodies to appraise and apply its general principles in the development of international law.[1]

THE PRACTICES OF STATES

During the proceedings before the International Court, Great Britain notified the Court that it would "naturally feel itself free to reconsider its policy" in the light of the forthcoming decision, particularly on the delimitation of the "rock-rampart" of the Scottish coast, by regarding the judgment as an authoritative "precedent for general application."[2] That the Court's pronouncement would be taken as just such a precedent became quickly evident. Some authorities were suggesting that the ruling be applied to the whole coast of Norway,[3] to the South Australian gulfs, which ranged more than one hundred miles in width, and to the Great Barrier Reefs of Australia, extending more than 1,000 miles from Cape York to Great Sandy Island.[4] Such proposals made clear the exceptional interest with which coastal states viewed the possible applications of the general principles of the Fisheries Case.

The Tidelands Oil Controversy.—In the Tidelands cases, the Supreme

1. Johnson, "Fisheries Case," p. 180.
2. Statement by Beckett, I.C.J., *Pleadings*, IV, 374. However, Great Britain considered in 1953 that the judgment, depending on its specific facts, was not to be taken as applicable to all or any other coast—see Selwyn Lloyd's statement in the *Times* (London), December 15, 1953.
3. Suggested by Evensen in "Fisheries Case," p. 628.
4. O'Connell, "Geneva Conference," pp. 135-36. Straight baselines were to be applied across Spencer Gulf and Encounter Bay; the waters between the Reefs and the mainland were to be claimed as internal sea, as with the Indreleia of Norway.

Court of the United States decided that the federal government had "the paramount rights and power" as to resources lying under the territorial sea, but left undisturbed the title of individual states to the beds of internal waters.[5] Consequently, the dividing line between the two seas, that is, the baseline for the territorial sea, became the focus of attention, involving the question of jurisdiction over vast amounts of offshore oil deposits. The states which stood to lose the fabulous riches of the tidelands to the federal government were eager somehow to enlarge the internal sea. But according to United States laws, the baseline was to be the low-water mark for normal coastlines, while the bays and islands were under the six-mile rule and the ten-mile rule, respectively.[6]

It was in the context of this controversy that the Fisheries Case came to play a significant role. In fact, even before the case was decided in the International Court, the California Legislature in 1951 adopted a liberal straight-baseline system,[7] in order to regain most of the contested areas between the United States and California. It was, however, Samuel W. Yorty, a California congressman, who initiated a movement to use the Fisheries Case in the Tidelands controversy. Yorty declared that the federal government's schemes "to deprive California of rights in State-owned submerged coastal lands have now been smashed by a decision of the International Court of Justice."[8]

Yorty's argument was that the Fisheries Case indicated that the United States' position was "not supported or required by international law," because "it was permissible under international law for Norway to use as its base line straight lines between the farthest off shore islands" and also because a claim to a bay as inland waters "depends on geographical and economic factors and on local special conditions." He concluded that the Court's judgment clearly established that "the United States can and, indeed, should make the determination in the light of its own best interests in regard to such factors as national security, economic requirements, international practice, geography, historical usages, and law enforcement." On February 11, 1952, Yorty introduced a joint resolution (H.J.R. 373) declaring the boundaries of the internal waters of the United States to be "as far seaward as is permissible under international law." He attempted to apply to the whole coast of the United

5. *U.S.* v. *California*, 332 U.S. 804 (1947); *U.S.* v. *Texas*, 340 U.S. 900 (1950); *U.S.* v. *Louisiana*, 340 U.S. 899 (1950); see Bartley, *Tidelands Oil Controversy*, for the historical and legal basis of these cases.

6. See the U.S. Department of Justice's contention to this effect, *Congressional Record*, 82d Cong., 2d Sess., 1952, XCVIII, Pt. 1, A 433, c. 3; 966-67, c. 3-c.1.

7. See California, *Government Code*, §§ 170, 171 (1951).

8. *Congressional Record*, 82d Cong., 2d Sess., 1952, XCVIII, Pt. 8, A 29, c.3.

States "a series of straight lines running between the headlands of all indentations" and "running around the outer edges of the farthest off-lying islands, rocks, and reefs," in terms of the basically subjective criteria enumerated in the Court's judgment.[9]

Yorty's purpose in attempting to give effect to the liberal principle of the Court's decision in the Fisheries Case was primarily to create for the individual states an enlarged internal sea, by extending seaward the baseline of the territorial sea. This scheme would also have created a vast new sphere of national territory, even if the three-mile limit for the extent of the territorial sea were retained. Before Yorty's resolution could be seriously considered, however, the federal government "returned" the sovereign rights over the territorial sea to the individual states by "quitclaim" legislation—the Submerged Land Act of 1953.[10] The impetus behind the Yorty Resolution quickly subsided, removing a potential source of international controversy.

The Anglo-Icelandic Fisheries Dispute.—In the United States the move to apply the implications of the Fisheries Case did not bring results. In Iceland, however, the government resolutely implemented a policy based on these implications, attracting the keen interest of many other maritime states.

Iceland, which with its coastal islands, islets, and skerries may properly be regarded as a mid-ocean archipelago, was heavily dependent upon fishing for its national livelihood. Even before the Fisheries Case, Iceland had been moving in the direction of an extended fishery zone. On April 5, 1948, a law concerning the "scientific conservation of the continental shelf fisheries" was proclaimed, empowering the Ministry of Fisheries to issue regulations establishing conservation zones within the limits of the continental shelf.[11] On April 22, 1950, the Ministry of Fisheries issued the first set of regulations prohibiting all trawling and Danish seine-netting in the area between Horn and Langanes on the north coast of Iceland, inside a line "four nautical miles from a base line drawn between the outermost points of the coast, islands and rocks and across the opening of bays."[12] Twelve base points were enumerated, the new line bearing a close resemblance to the line delimited by the Norwegian Royal Decree of July 12, 1935.

The British government objected, and, after an exchange of notes, Iceland announced its readiness to maintain the status quo with regard

9. *Ibid.*, Pt. 1, A 343-44. c.3-c.1; 967-68; c.3-c.1.
10. 67 Stat. 29; 43 U.S.C. 1301-15 (1953).
11. Iceland, *Icelandic Efforts for Fisheries Conservation*, Appendix A, pp. 28-30.
12. Section 1 of the regulations, *ibid.*, Appendix B, p. 31.

to British vessels after October 3, 1951, when the new regulations would have gone into effect. The hope was that the Fisheries Case, then pending, would provide an answer to the legal questions involved in the Icelandic practice.[13] During the case hearings, the British spokesman, Sir Eric Beckett, made explicit to the Court the fact that the case was important not only to the two litigants, but to the parties in other possible disputes as well. He mentioned specifically the Icelandic case.[14]

On March 19, 1952, only three months after the Court's judgment was delivered, Iceland instituted new regulations, not only confirming the four-mile limit of the territorial sea and the baseline system of the 1950 regulations, but also carrying the system around the entire coast of the islands, with 48 base points in all.[15] The longest baselines were 66 and 41 miles, across the Faxa Floi and Breidifjord, respectively.

The British government, serving notice on May 2, 1952, expressed opposition to both the four-mile rule and the "extreme line" of straight baselines chosen by the Icelandic government.[16] The British based their contention on the traditional concept of the extent of the territorial sea as three miles unless there be "very exceptional historic ground," as in the case of Norway; and on the finding in the Fisheries Case that "the delimitation of sea areas has always an international aspect; it cannot be dependent merely upon the will of the coastal State." The choice of a baseline, the British argued, was governed by the "three elements" expressed in the Court's judgment. Therefore, they concluded, the line across the Faxa Floi—18 miles longer than the longest line prescribed by the Norwegian decree of 1935—could not be justified.[17]

On the other hand, Iceland, in conformity with the liberal "general criteria formulated by the International Court,"[18] based its argument on the geographical and economic "realities" of the island country. It

13. Statement by Olafur Thors, Minister of Industries, *ibid.*, Appendix H, pp. 55-56; see also Johnson, "Icelandic Fishery's Limits," pp. 72-73.

14. I.C.J., *Pleadings*, IV, 37; see also p. 23 for Soskice's statement to the same effect.

15. Article 1 of the regulations, *Icelandic Efforts for Fisheries Conservation*, Appendix C, p. 33.

16. *Ibid.*, Appendix D, pp. 37-39.

17. *Ibid.*, pp. 38-39. The three elements were explained: "(1) The principle that 'the drawing of the base lines must not depart to any appreciable extent from the general direction of the coast.' (2) The principle that the sea areas lying within the base lines must be 'sufficiently closely linked to the land domain to be subject to the regime of internal waters.' (3) The principle that, even though it may be lawful to draw base lines across sea areas not falling within the conception of a bay, the sea areas across which the base lines are drawn should be situated *inter fauces terrarum*."

18. *Ibid.*, pp. 22-23; for a better analysis of such criteria see a *note verbale*, March 25, 1955, in *Report of I.L.C.*, 10th Sess., p. 29.

41

pointed out the "overexploitation resulting in a complete exhaustion of fishing grounds"[19] and its total dependence on the coastal fisheries and the exports of fishery products amounting to "97% of the total exports of Iceland"—that is, "a matter of life or death."[20] Liberally applying the rule of *inter fauces terrarum*, Iceland further asserted that the Faxa Floi line was "adapted to 'practical needs and local requirements' without departing to any appreciable extent from the general direction of the coast,"[21] and thus it was "reasonable" and "moderate," as in the case of the Lopphavet basin of Norway in which the Court upheld a long baseline across the basin on almost purely geographical grounds.

Iceland presented its concept of a bay in the same light. Referring to the Court's rejection of the ten-mile rule and its justification of drawing straight baselines even across "minor curvatures" for convenience, Iceland asserted that "the question of bays does not call for special rules in the case of coastlines which are indented" and "the drawing of baselines in that case would be governed by the general principles" which could be adapted to specific conditions.[22]

Furthermore, in its argument for the four-mile limit of the territorial sea, Iceland declared that "the so-called 3-mile rule has no authority under international law any more than the so-called 10-mile rule in bays which was firmly rejected by the Court,"[23] and that "the practice of states seems to be incompatible with the acceptance of a general rule fixing the extent of the territorial sea with precision."[24] Upon these considerations, the Icelandic government asserted that "each State may within reasonable limits itself determine the extent of its jurisdiction over coastal fisheries in view of local economic, geographic, biological and relevant considerations."[25] Notable is the complete disregard of historic titles. In this respect, therefore, Iceland's position is more nearly in

19. The Presidential Proclamation of April 5, 1948, *Icelandic Efforts for Fisheries Conservation*, p. 29.

20. Statement by Gudmundur I. Gudmundsson, Foreign Minister, in U.N. Press and Publications Division, Office of Public Information, *Press Release*, PM/3650, September 24, 1958, pp. 10-11; see also Iceland, *Icelandic Fisheries Limits*, pp. 10-12.

21. Note from Iceland to Great Britain, May 21, 1952, in *Icelandic Efforts for Fisheries Conservation*, Appendix D (2), p. 40; cf. I.C.J., *Reports*, p. 133, on the Lopphavet case.

22. Iceland's reply to the I.L.C. in 1955, *A.J.I.L.*, L (1956), Off. Doc., Annex, pp. 248-49; cf. I.C.J., *Reports*, pp. 129-30, 131.

23. *Icelandic Efforts for Fisheries Conservation*, Appendix D (2), p. 41; cf. I.C.J., *Reports*, p. 131.

24. *A.J.I.L.*, L (1956), Off. Doc., Annex, p. 131.

25. *Icelandic Efforts for Fisheries Conservation*, Appendix D (2), p. 41, (4), p. 43; cf. Alvarez' opinion, I.C.J., *Reports*, p. 150.

accord with Alvarez' concurring opinion in the Fisheries Case than with the Court's majority opinion.

Iceland thus applied the Court's judgment to its own needs, giving full effect to the general criteria enunciated in it. It is not surprising, therefore, that the judgment was viewed as giving "a general blessing"[26] to the baseline system in the case of indented coasts.

With the initial issue still unresolved, the Anglo-Icelandic dispute was further aggravated by a new set of regulations promulgated by Iceland on June 30, 1958, which superseded the previous set. The new regulations expanded the limits of the fishery zone from four to twelve miles, based on the same base points and baselines used in the 1952 regulations. Iceland justified this move by claiming that it conformed to "practical needs and local requirements."[27] In protesting against the new regulations, Great Britain countered by sending her gunboats to escort her fishing fleet within the twelve-mile limit. Iceland reaffirmed its stand, arguing that "hard and fast rules do not exist in international law" concerning the delimitation of coastal waters and that "features of a geographical, economical, political, and historical nature specific for Iceland and for Iceland alone" must be taken into account.[28]

Developments in the Icelandic fisheries jurisdiction question alone are sufficient to show that the liberal and subjective principles of the Fisheries Case outweigh by far the Court's reference to "an international aspect" of delimitation and the role of historic titles, however diminished in significance they might be. In actual practice, the latter seems to be a most fragile safeguard, indeed.

Latin American Fisheries and Maritime Zones.—Since World War II Argentina, Mexico, Panama, Chile, Peru, Ecuador, Costa Rica, Honduras, Nicaragua, and El Salvador, respectively, have extended their jurisdiction, if not sovereignty, over the vast superjacent waters of the continental shelf, specifically for fishery purposes. The decision in the Fisheries Case was taken by some authorities to provide a new justification for this vast expansionist tendency. This view was well expressed by Andrés A. Aramburú y Menchaca who presented an official report of the Bar Association of Lima, Peru, to the Fourth Conference of the International Bar Association held at Madrid, Spain, in 1952. As the International Court allegedly acknowledged in the Fisheries Case, he asserted, "it is not necessary" to fix a uniform rule for all countries, and "it is possible to fix territorial waters of different extensions according

26. Johnson, "Icelandic Fishery's Limits," p. 351.
27. Iceland, *British Aggression in Icelandic Waters*, Appendix B, pp. 29-32.
28. Statement by Gudmundsson, U.N., *Press Release*, PM/3650, 1958, p. 15.

to the geographical position of the countries" which would "satisfy the requirements of the right of preservation to its full extent."[29] Aramburú y Menchaca in this statement obviously alluded to the Court's implication that there existed no hard and fast rules for the delimitation of the territorial sea. Or rather he completely equated the Court's judgment with Alvarez' succinct concurring opinion.

His main tenet was firmly accepted by Latin American countries in the famous "Principles of Mexico," which were adopted by the Inter-American Council of Jurists at Mexico City in 1956, as "the expression of the juridical conscience of the Continent, and as applicable between the American States."[30] Significantly, it was reported that in the meeting "the participants endorsed the thesis upheld by Dr. Alejandro Alvarez in his individual opinion in the *Anglo-Norwegian Fisheries Case.*"[31] In this spirit, the Principles, recognizing that "the distance of three miles as the limit of territorial waters is insufficient," adopted a resolution that "each state is competent to establish its territorial waters within reasonable limits, taking into account geographical, geological, and biological factors, as well as the economic needs of its population, and its security and defense."[32] Subsequently, Latin American delegations to international bodies have most consistently upheld this stand.[33]

Another point in the Alvarez opinion which had considerable appeal for the Latin American countries was that which stressed a regional approach. Alvarez, specifically mentioning the recent development among Latin American countries of a continental approach to fishery conservation, emphasized that such rights were "of great weight if established by a group of States, and especially by all the States of a continent."[34] Aramburú y Menchaca echoed Alvarez' regional approach to contiguous zones in different geographic zones.[35] The regional approach was also

29. "Character and Scope of the Rights," pp. 122-23.
30. *Inter-American Juridical Yearbook*, 1956-57, p. 227.
31. Statement of the Secretary of the Commission on the Proceedings of the Third Meeting of the Inter-American Council of Jurists, in *Yearbook of I.L.C.*, *1956*, II, 240; cf. Alvarez' opinion in I.C.J., *Reports*, p. 150.
32. *Inter-American Juridical Yearbook*, 1956-57, p. 227. The U.S. almost alone refrained from voting with the majority, declaring that "much of the Resolution is contrary to international law" and that it was "clearly designed to serve political purposes" (p. 239).
33. See statements by Luis Melo Lecaros (Chile) in U.N. Gen. Ass. *Official Records*, 11th Sess., 1956, Sixth Committee (A/C.6/SR.496), p. 85; Luis Padilla-Nervo (Mexico) in *Yearbook of I.L.C.*, *1956*, I, 171-72; F. V. Garcia Amador (Cuba), *ibid.*, pp. 179-80; Isidore Ruiz Moreno (Argentina) in U.N. Conference on the Law of the Sea, *Official Records*, III, 42.
34. I.C.J., *Reports*, p. 150.
35. "Character and Scope," p. 123.

reflected in the Santiago Declaration of 1952. With this document Chile, Ecuador, and Peru established a joint Maritime Zone with a 200-mile limit for mutual protection of "irreplaceable sources of subsistence and vital economic resources."[36]

In the light of the above cited developments, it is clear that the application by the Latin American states of the principles of the Fisheries Case has been more than liberal. Alvarez' concurring opinion in particular was utilized to the fullest. So ready were these states to invoke the principles of vital economic and social interests and of practical needs and local requirements, that the concepts of reasonableness, moderation, and adaptability of the general principles of international law were in danger of being stretched to the point of meaninglessness. The Syngman Rhee Line, claimed by Korea, is perhaps another example of such exaggerated claims. Enunciated on January 18, 1952, this line extended Korea's seaward territorial jurisdiction for fishery and security purposes, quite substantially: 50 to 60 miles.[37]

The Indonesian and Philippine Archipelagos.—The Indonesian archipelago, a group of some 13,000 islands scattered over a vast area of the sea, is a strategically located oceanic archipelago at the crossing point of the Pacific, the South China Sea, and the Indian Ocean. The Indonesian government on December 13, 1957, claimed "all waters around, between and connecting the islands or parts of islands belonging to the Indonesian archipelago, irrespective of their width or dimension" as "natural appurtenances of its land territorial" and thus an integral part of the national waters subject to the absolute sovereignty of Indonesia.[38] In addition, the government expanded its territorial sea to 12 miles measured from straight baselines drawn between the outermost points of all the islands and islets, many of which are more than 100 miles long.[39]

Indonesia justified this claim on the basis of its essential role in creating national unity, its conformity to geographical conditions, the need to suppress smuggling and piracy, and the requirements of national de-

36. *Yearbook of I.L.C., 1956*, I, 169; Costa Rica joined by signing the Protocol of Accession at Quito on October 5, 1955; see also Bayitch, *Interamerican Law*, pp. 42-47, for the tripartite conventions of 1956.

37. See *United Nations, Legislative Series, Laws and Regulations on the Territorial Sea*, 1957, pp. 30-31; see the U.S.-Mexican shrimp problem, in Svarlien, "Territorial Sea," p. 346n71; the Soviet fisheries policy as decreed in 1956, and the Chinese claim to the East China Sea, in Oda, *International Law of the Sea*, pp. 81-82, 133-49, 120-21.

38. See Great Britain, *Territorial Sea*, pp. 8-9.

39. See comments justifying the "unilateral act" in Pakasi, "Indonesia and the Geneva Conference," p. 17.

fense.[40] To bolster her use of the straight-baseline method, Indonesia sought support in the principles of the Fisheries Case and asserted that in adopting the baseline system "Indonesia does not stand alone."[41]

It is true that the International Court rejected the ten-mile rule for straight baselines drawn across bays and between islands and islets and stressed the liberal application of water-crossing lines with due regard to local conditions and requirements. It is also true, however, that in any given case, according to the Court, the more or less close dependence of the territorial sea upon the land domain must remain of paramount importance, and the drawing of the baselines must not depart to any appreciable extent from the general direction of the coast of the archipelago viewed as a whole.[42] From this point of view, exorbitantly long baselines, enclosing vast areas of sea from free navigation and fishing and forming a sort of Indonesian lake, could hardly come within the terms of "reasonableness" and "moderation," however liberally the subjective criteria of the Fisheries Case might be interpreted.[43] In this case again Alvarez' concurring opinion seems to be equated with the Court's majority opinion by disregarding completely historic factors and international concern.

The Philippine government has made claims similar to those of Indonesia. It considers that its territorial domain extends over "all waters around, between and connecting different islands belonging to the Philippine Archipelago, irrespective of their width or dimension."[44] Although it is not known to what extent the authorities recognize free navigation for foreign ships through the numerous passages of the archipelago, it is clear that the archipelago, composed of some 7,100 islands, scattered over a large expanse of water, is regarded, like the Indonesian, as a political and legal unit connected by a series of imaginary straight baselines.[45]

40. See the *Times* (London), December 16, 1957, p. 8, December 19,1957, p. 9; the *New York Times*, January 18, 1958, p. 3; see also a statement by A. Sunario, Indonesian Ambassador at London, in the *Times* (London), December 19, 1957, p. 10.

41. Pakasi, "Indonesia and the Geneva Conference," p. 17.

42. See I.C.J., *Reports*, pp. 131, 133, 141.

43. For criticism to this effect see the *Times* (London), December 16, 1957, p. 7; statement by Arthur H. Dean in U.N. Conference on the Law of the Sea, *Official Records*, III, 25-26.

44. See *note verbale*, March 7, 1955, in *Report of I.L.C.*, 10th Sess., pp. 36-37; see also McDougal and Burke, *Public Order*, p. 315n29, for Philippine Republic Act No. 3046, approved June 17, 1961.

45. Jens Evensen, "Certain Legal Aspects Concerning the Delimitation of the Territorial Waters of Archipelagos," Preparatory Doc. No. 15 in U.N. Conference on the Law of the Sea, *Official Documents*, I, 299.

Peter the Great Bay.—The Soviet claim to Peter the Great Bay as part of its territorial sea came on July 20, 1957, when the Council of Ministers of the Soviet Union ordered that the boundary in that area be measured from a straight baseline, approximately 115 miles long, running from the estuary of the River Tyumen-Ula and the Provorotny promontory. The decree was immediately followed by protests from Japan and the United States that the closure of the Bay was "contrary to international law," and that it encroached upon "the well-established principle of freedom of the sea."[46]

In its reply, the Soviet government argued that the waters of the bay are "historically waters of the Soviet Union by force of the special geographic conditions of that bay and its special economic and defense significance." Although the Russians referred to Peter the Great Bay as a historic bay, their argument is more consistent with the "vital bay" concept.[47] It is well known that in the bay is Vladivostok, the sole naval establishment of the Soviet Union's Maritime Province, operating all year and now equipped with guided missile bases.[48] The bay is also a famous fishing ground for flatfish and cod and as such has frequently led to disputes between Russia and Japan.[49] The Soviet argument, therefore, is very reminiscent of the Norwegian contention in the Fisheries Case which stressed "legitimate interests" and cited the historic factor only as a supplementary element. The International Court's decision, furthermore, was so emphatic on the significant roles played by economic, geographic, and social criteria in resolving problems of the territorial sea that there was really no need to adduce the historic factor.[50]

The Soviets continued their argument for enclosing the bay in a note of January 7, 1958. Although Peter the Great Bay is actually composed of several bays, and includes many scattered islands, islets, and reefs, the Soviets claimed that the nature of the "whole coastline surrounding this bay, which is deeply indented in the continent," and the "very configuration of the bay" show that "it comprises an inseparable whole with

46. Iriye, "Peter the Great Bay," p. 1166; see also *New York Times*, July 21, 1957, p. 1; "U.S. Protests to U.S.S.R.," p. 388.
47. "Soviet Note of January 7," p. 461; see the Soviet claim to the "natural and other special conditions" in the transcription of the Moscow Radio Broadcast of August 7, 1957, in Uchida, "Soviet Legal Theory," p. 935.
48. As reported in the *Times* (London), August 19, 1957, p. 12.
49. Thus three agreements (in 1907, 1928, and 1949) were concluded, concerning the Japanese right to fish within the bay. In the agreements the bay was delimited by straight baselines drawn "from Cape Provorotni to Cape Gamova, including the islands situated in that bay"—Iriye, p. 1166.
50. See I.C.J., *Pleadings*, II, 133, for the Norwegian argument; cf. I.C.J., *Reports*, pp. 133, 138, 139, 142, 152, for historic titles considered with other criteria.

47

the Soviet dry land territory."[51] In the Fisheries Case the Court had enumerated two geographical criteria which would seem relevant to this claim: there must be a "close dependence of the territorial sea upon the land domain," and the baselines must be "sufficiently closely linked to the land domain" in order to be "subject to the regime of internal waters," or *inter fauces terrarum*. Yet in application of these principles to define the Svaerholthavet basin—where a number of baselines could be drawn because there were several bays and scattered islands in the geographical configuration—the Court argued that the general direction of the coast rule is "devoid of any mathematical precision" and that "the coastal State would seem to be in the best position to appraise the local conditions dictating the selection."[52] Hence, the coastal states in such cases were allowed discretion to draw their straight baselines wherever they wished, in the light of the purely geographical factors alone.

In the light of this decision by the Court, it would seem to be at the discretion of the Soviet authorities whether they treat Peter the Great Bay as a unit or as several bays. When the local conditions of the bay are appraised in terms of the military, economic, and geographical factors advanced by the Soviet government, it becomes difficult indeed to deny the legitimacy of the Soviet claim to the bay, with or without historic title.

Conclusion.—All of these developments have one thing in common: an almost total lack of regard for the "international aspect" of the problems of delimitation and territorial jurisdiction. Each state seems to have taken to itself the right to decide what its delimitation should be, allowing its self-interest full expression in terms of the liberal criteria inferred from the Fisheries Case, or rather from Alvarez' concurring opinion which interprets the problems of delimitation and the extent of seaward jurisdiction as almost purely of domestic and subjective concern. This is particularly true as regards the question of extent of the territorial sea. Since 1951 some twenty-one states have extended their territorial seas, so that they ranged from 5 to 12 miles.[53] Significantly, all of them are either small Western nations or among the newly emerging nations. It appears to be clear that among other factors which may be said to have had a more or less general influence in determining the positions of the various nations is a general aversion to the three-mile limit as an alleged reminder of colonial domination in the name

51. "Soviet Note of January 7," p. 462; contrast with the U.S. protest note dated March 6, 1958, in the same vol., p. 461.
52. I.C.J., *Reports*, pp. 133, 141; see also Johnson, "Fisheries Case," pp. 67-68.
53. See below, Appendix II; 1 state claims 5 miles; 4 claim 6; 1 claims 10; and 15 claim 12.

48

of the freedom of the seas.[54] It is true that, traditionally, the strongest supporters of the three-mile limit and a narrower territorial expanse have been Great Britain and the United States, closely followed by Japan, Germany, and other Western nations. In this sense, too, the general aversion to the principle of historic titles and exception, which inevitably works in favor of the traditional maritime powers, is understandable. Thus, the general spirit of the Court in the Fisheries Case, augmented and accentuated by Alvarez' opinion, could be readily acceptable as justifying a forceful way of asserting the won independence of the smaller and emerging nations as well as the causes of the dissatisfied nations in the traditionally Western community of nations, such as the Latin American countries.

THE INTERNATIONAL LAW COMMISSION AND THE GENEVA CONFERENCES

Despite its astute approach to the problems of modern international law, the Court's judgment in the Fisheries Case, accentuated by Alvarez' concurring opinion, left certain disturbingly subjective elements in the law, which could, and in fact did, contribute to a chaotic situation in the development of the law. As already observed, Alvarez' opinion, if readily applied with discretion, will be tantamount to the destruction of the whole concept of freedom of the seas. Elasticity and flexibility are desirable and truly necessary for a living customary law. Yet, to have meaning they must operate within an objective system of standards and principles. The Court's judgment did give recognition to the principles of order and basic uniformity, but the effect was insignificant in the context of the liberal character of the general criteria and other subjective elements. In this respect, "unless international law provides for the obligation of the coastal State to submit to impartial determination," as one authority puts it, "the general rule laid down by the Court—being dependent for its operation solely upon the will of the coastal State—does not seem to measure up to an essential requirement of a legal rule."[55]

Although the Court did not lay down objective standards, neither did it imply that there was no more place for international law in questions of the sea or that each nation should decide all such questions unilaterally. The Court did provide a set of guiding principles for a progressive development of international law, acknowledging that the future of the law depended not only on the decision itself, but "on the reception

54. See Sorensen, "Law of the Sea," p. 245, for his observation on the general attitude of these nations at the Geneva Conference in 1958.
55. Lauterpacht, *International Law*, p. 198.

given to it by governments and by international bodies."[56] These principles were destined to be significant in the further work of the International Law Commission and the United Nations General Assembly on the codification of the law of the seas within the mid-twentieth-century frame.

In this section we shall examine the impact of the Court's judgment and the recent developments in state practice upon the work of the International Law Commission and the Geneva Conferences on the Law of the Sea (1958 and 1960), whose membership was almost twice the number of sovereign states at the Hague Conference of 1930. We shall give particular attention to how much these international bodies were able to lend precision and uniformity to the general principles of the Fisheries Case, with reference to traditional concepts and state practice.

Baseline Concept.—Despite his acknowledgment that the Fisheries Case was an authoritative pronouncement "approved by a substantial majority of the Court," J. P. A. François, the Special Rapporteur of the International Law Commission, considered the Commission's task to be the "progressive development" of international law as well as of codification of existing law. In this spirit he proposed as the general rule, in his first draft (Article 5), the low-water mark or the coastal rule, and the straight-baseline system as a special case for deeply or heavily indented coasts and for those with a group of islands. Only in the latter case did he insert two criteria from the Fisheries Case: "The drawing of baselines must not depart to any appreciable extent from the general direction of the coasts," and "the sea areas lying within these lines must be sufficiently closely linked to the land domain to be subject to the regime of internal waters."[57]

This conservative attitude of François toward the straight-baseline system was even more apparent in his third report, which departed most radically from the major implications of the Fisheries Case on three counts: first, by the use of the "largest-scale chart available" for delimitation, rejecting any latitude in the local conditions provided for in the Court's judgment;[58] second, by the provision of ten miles as the "maximum permissible length for a 'straight baseline'"[59] between

56. Johnson, "Fisheries Case," p. 180.

57. *Yearbook of I.L.C., 1952,* I, 143, II, 35, 32-33 (Article 5).

58. See Article 5 in U.N. Gen. Ass., *Official Records,* 11th Sess., Annex, Agenda 53 (A/C.6/L.378) (1956), p. 9 (hereafter cited as Agenda 53); cf. I.C.J., *Reports,* p. 141. This revised report was primarily based on the recommendations of the Committee of Experts.

59. Agenda 53, p. 9; cf. I.C.J., *Reports,* p. 134; see also criticism of the revised report by Norway, Iceland, and Sweden in *A.J.I.L.,* L (1956), Off. Doc. (A/2934), Annex, pp. 248-49, 263-64, 270; hereafter cited as *A.J.I.L.,* L.

islands; and third, by a rule that "baselines shall not be drawn to and from drying rocks and shoals."[60]

Manley O. Hudson, opposing the François report, argued that "it was open to States to adopt the approach advocated by the Court" by taking into account "economic considerations." J. M. Yepes asserted in the same spirit that "some flexible formula would have to be sought which would be applicable as appropriate to each case."[61]

Under such criticism for departing from the Fisheries Case, the Commission in its 1955 draft modified its stand substantially on four major points. First, the phrase "as an exception" relating to the use of straight baselines was deleted because it appeared to have "no legal relevance in the context." Second, the ten-mile rule was taken out "so as not to make the provisions too mechanical" and arbitrary. Third, and most drastic, an additional criterion for delimitation included in the Fisheries Case was inserted: "Where this is justified by economic interests peculiar to a region, the reality and importance of which are clearly evidenced by a long usage, the base line may be independent of the low-water mark." The fourth change was the deletion of "historical reasons" for the exceptional use of straight baselines, as if to emphasize economic, geographical, and social factors in conformity with the criteria established by the Court.[62]

In the 1956 session of the Commission, however, the provision of "economic interest" as a criterion for justifying the use of a straight-baseline system met strong opposition from Great Britain, Belgium, and the United States.[63] A. E. F. Sandstrom, summarizing the opposition, asserted that according to the Court's opinion in the Fisheries Case, the application of a straight-baseline system was held "justified in principle on other grounds [historic and geographical factors] before purely local economic considerations could justify a particular way of drawing the lines."[64] The Commission accepted this interpretation and in its final draft of 1956 discarded economic interests as a factor in justifying the straight-baseline system and relegated economic considerations to a secondary place. This was a significant departure from the Court's judgment, for, as S. B. Krylov correctly observed, "economic interests" with

60. Agenda 53, p. 10; see *A.J.I.L.*, L, 264, for the Norwegian comment that the Court approved the Norwegian delimitation of "straight baselines which had drying rocks and shoals for points of departure."

61. *Yearbook of I.L.C., 1952*, I, 172-73, 174.

62. See Article 5 of the draft, in Agenda 53, p. 10; *A.J.I.L.*, L, 244; see also p. 225 for the Commission's acceptance of the Court's judgment as an authoritative pronouncement.

63. See "Comments by Certain Governments," pp. 996, 1023, 1043.

64. Agenda 53, p. 10.

local latitude if applied in a "reasonable and moderate manner" was considered essentially equal to geographical considerations in the Fisheries Case.[65]

This conservative attitude of the majority of the Commission is understandable in the light of several already discussed extravagant developments in expanding the territorial limit by liberally interpreting the general criteria of the Fisheries Case or rather by elevating Judge Alvarez' opinion to the level of the majority opinion. The Commission's task was to set forth concrete and uniform objective rules of law for codification, and thus it was inevitably directed to weaken, if not to emasculate, the basically subjective tendency of those developments.

The final draft of the Commission, with the greatly minimized role of "economic interests," was accepted in principle by the Geneva Conference on the Law of the Sea in 1958.[66]

The crucial point in the First Committee of the Geneva Conference was whether to adopt a maximum distance for straight baselines. Great Britain proposed a maximum distance of ten miles. The Soviet Union, on the other hand, opposing any mechanical limit, asserted that the final draft of the International Law Commission "constituted a better safeguard of the interests of the coastal State." The Indian delegation, quoting from the Fisheries Case in the same spirit, suggested that straight baselines without any maximum limit must be instituted, even "in minor curvatures of the coastlines." Sweden proposed an amendment to the British proposal, allowing for a fifteen-mile maximum. Great Britain accepted this amendment and the First Committee adopted the amended motion as a compromise.[67]

In the plenary meetings of the Conference, however, Canada asserted that such an arbitrary mathematical limit was "neither necessary nor desirable" under the principle of the general direction of the coast and in the light of the Fisheries Case. Supported strongly by the Soviet Union and Indonesia, the Canadian motion to delete the maximum length for straight baselines altogether was adopted.[68]

65. Agenda 53, p. 188; see in Chap. 3 above, "The Rule of the General Direction of the Coast."

66. See Article 4 in Appendix III, below.

67. U.N. Conference on the Law of the Sea, *Official Records* (hereafter cited as Conference *Official Records*), I, 148, 156-59, 161, 228, 252, 258 (see also pp. 156, 252, for the proposal on the 10-mile limit endorsed by Germany, Greece, Italy, and Japan). The vote was 44 to 0 with 31 abstentions.

68. Conference *Official Records*, II, 62; the vote was 35 to 31 with 10 abstentions. Article 4 in its final form was thus adopted, 62 to 8, with 8 abstentions; only Uruguay, Belgium, France, Germany, Japan, Luxemburg, Monaco, and the Netherlands opposed (p. 65).

Although the fifteen-mile maximum was thus removed, an examination of Articles 4 and 5 of the final draft shows that the implications of the Fisheries Case were by no means fully relied upon. First, the role of "economic interests," "practical needs and local requirements," and "local latitude" in selection of base points and baselines, is reduced to determination of particular baselines rather than providing justification for an overall baselines system.[69] Second, the straight-baseline system in "the general direction of the coast" rule itself has lost much of its vitality, because of the acceptance of the "low-water mark" rule as the general rule. Third, drying rocks or low-tide elevations are rejected as points of departure for straight baselines.[70] Finally, the status of the areas of water which may be enclosed between the coast and the baselines is now regarded in Article 5 as identical to that of the territorial sea in which the right of innocent passage is permitted, thus discarding the Court's opinion on the Indreleia of Norway as "internal waters" subject to the sovereignty of the coastal state.[71]

By no means, however, did the Conference revert to the law of delimitation at the Hague Conference of 1930—the rule of the low-water mark. In attempts to stem the tide of the exaggerated application of the principles of the Fisheries Case and to mold the principles into a more objective set of standard and uniform rules, the International Law Commission and the Geneva Conference adopted a rather conservative attitude. Yet no rigid and mechanical rules for the straight-baseline system were accepted and, by the use of such geographical terms as "deeply indented," "any appreciable extent," "sufficiently closely linked," and even by the concept of the "general direction of the coast" itself, the Conference left considerable room for flexible application. It might be said that while the Fisheries Case was thus kept from unduly upsetting the framework of traditional concepts, the impetus it had given to the bringing about of needed changes in terms of present world conditions was maintained by the subsequent work of the International Law Commission and the Geneva Conference of 1958.

Islands, Archipelagos, and Drying Rocks and Shoals.—The Court in the Fisheries Case approved the liberal application of straight baselines not only across bays but also "between islands, islets and rocks, across the sea area separating them."[72] The International Law Commission,

69. For a more analytical essay see Fitzmaurice, "Results of the Geneva Conference," pp. 76-78.
70. See the Norwegian protest based on the Fisheries Case against this rule, Conference *Official Records*, II, 63.
71. Article 5 in Appendix III, below.
72. I.C.J., *Reports*, p. 130.

on the other hand, refused to lump together islands and rocks, preferring to make careful distinctions. The problems of islands and drying rocks or low-tide elevations were treated in three separate articles. First, it was decided (Article 4) that when certain enumerated geographic conditions permit the use of straight baselines between islands, it is nevertheless unlawful to use drying rocks or shoals as "terminal points" or departing points of baselines.[73] Second, it was provided (Article 11) that drying rocks or shoals "wholly or partially within the territorial sea, as measured from the mainland or an island, may be taken as points of departure for measuring the extension of the territorial sea." In short, drying rocks or shoals could only be used once in measuring the outer limit of the territorial sea. Third, an island was defined (Article 10) as "an area of land, surrounded by water, which in normal circumstances is permanently above high-water" and as possessing "its own territorial sea," thus excluding drying rocks or low-water elevations which are rocks above sea level only at the low tide.[74]

These clear distinctions between an island and a drying rock and between a drying rock admitted as a point of departure for the measurement of the territorial sea and that not allowed as a base point are obviously in contrast with the Court's judgment. The Court sanctioned the use of "drying rocks and shoals for points of departure" in straight baselines without regard to their size and location.[75] The final draft of the Commission was accepted in this respect without any change in substance,[76] greatly reducing the general latitude of the coastal states in selecting the base points for their delimitation of the extent of the territorial sea.

Another significant problem was the delimitation of the territorial sea of a group of islands, or an archipelago, both coastal and oceanic. This was a key issue particularly because of the development of exorbitant claims, such as those of the Indonesian and Philippine archipelagos, in the application of the straight-baseline system. Although the Court in the Fisheries Case pointed out that the principle of archipelagos had "not got beyond the stage of proposals," it sanctioned the application of a general principle of the general direction of the coast, with the flexible

73. *Yearbook of I.L.C., 1954*, I, 83 (Article 5 in the draft); however, exceptions will be the drying rocks and shoals with "lighthouses or similar installations which are permanently above sea level"—Article 4(3) in Appendix III, below.

74. *Report of I.L.C.*, 11th Sess., p. 17.

75. So argued Norway in its protest against the Commission's rigid distinctions, Conference *Official Records*, II, 63.

76. See Agenda 53, pp. 14-15, for the final draft of 1956; see also Conference *Official Records*, III, 186-87, 201, 259; Appendix III, below.

geographic and economic criteria "valid for any delimitation of the territorial sea."[77]

The International Law Commission in its treatment of the baseline concept (Article 5, or Article 4 in the final form) allowed straight baselines to be applied to a coastal archipelago or "a fringe of islands along the coast in its immediate vicinity,"[78] even though the "economic interests" factor was given a secondary role in deciding the baseline system. But the Commission declared that "the general rule will normally apply to other islands forming a group."[79] This meant that oceanic archipelagos would be subject to the low-water-mark rule.

This discrimination of the oceanic archipelago from the coastal archipelago was immediately challenged by the Danish and Icelandic governments which, citing the Fisheries Case, claimed that the general criteria formulated by the Court should be applied to "any delimitation of the territorial sea."[80] In its final draft, therefore, the Commission declared that it was "prevented from stating an opinion" on oceanic archipelagos by disagreement on the extent of the territorial sea, and added that it also lacked technical information on the subject.[81]

At the Geneva Conference of 1958, the Indonesian and Philippine delegations proposed that an oceanic archipelago must be treated as "a single geographic or economic unit" and that straight baselines be drawn "along the coast of outermost islands, following the general configuration of the archipelago." Czechoslovakia even urged taking into account the special position of island states, "justified on geographical, economic and security grounds." But the prevailing opinion at the Conference apparently favored continued customary development of prescriptions concerning oceanic archipelagos. Hence, without delving into all suggestions for the liberal application of the general principles of delimitation as enumerated in the Fisheries Case, the Conference decided that the matter required "further study," as suggested by Sir Gerald Fitzmaurice.[82]

Bays, General and Historic.—It will be recalled that the Court in the Fisheries Case appeared to have "abolished altogether the legal concept of a bay," in its rejection of the ten-mile rule, or any mathematical rule for that matter, under the rule of the general direction of the coast, and

77. I.C.J., *Reports*, p. 131.
78. See Article 4(1) in Appendix III, below.
79. *Report of I.L.C.*, 10th Sess., p. 18.
80. Conference *Official Records*, I, 82; *A.J.I.L.*, L, 249, 264.
81. *Yearbook of I.L.C., 1956*, II, 270.
82. Conference *Official Records*, III, 15, 239, 61, 163 (order of quotations); see p. 239 for the Yugoslav proposal for the general application of the straight-baseline system to oceanic as well as to coastal archipelagos. Article 10, without any provision for oceanic archipelagos, was adopted, 62 to 0, with 1 abstention.

also in its acceptance of straight baselines used even "in cases of minor curvatures of the coast line."[83] Nevertheless, François, considering that the Commission's task was one of the progressive development of international law, proposed that the ten-mile rule be adopted[84] and offered a technical definition of a bay in the juridical sense as a body whose "area is as large as, or larger than that of the semi-circle drawn on the entrance of that bay." His proposal was aimed at "salvaging" the legal concept of a bay itself.[85]

The ten-mile rule was opposed by a majority in the Commission.[86] But in spite of F. V. Garcia Amador's spirited objection to any mathematical criterion which he said was ruled out "in the spirit, if not the letter of the judgment of the International Court,"[87] a majority expressed itself in favor of a twenty-five-mile rule, particularly because "a limitation based on geographical and other considerations, which would be necessarily vague, would not suffice."[88] In the final draft of 1956, however, this figure was reduced to fifteen miles.[89]

Despite the disagreement on the width of bays, it is extremely significant to note that the Commission as a whole accepted the François definition of a bay, exempting such a bay from the merely exceptional application of the straight-baseline system as provided for in Article 5 (Article 4 in the final form).[90] Thus the Commission accepted the British concept of a bay put forward in the Fisheries Case as "a well-marked indentation whose penetration inland is in such proportion to the width of its mouth as to contain land-locked waters and constitute more than a mere curvature of the coast."[91] Here again is a clear indica-

83. See H. Lauterpacht's analysis to this effect in *Yearbook of I.L.C.*, *1952*, I, 188; I.C.J., *Reports*, pp. 129-30, 131.

84. See his statement to this effect in *Yearbook of I.L.C.*, *1952*, II, 35.

85. See the text of François' second report, based on the opinion of the Committee of Experts, in Agenda 53, pp. 11-12(n15); Lauterpacht's appreciation to François for his efforts is in *Yearbook of I.L.C.*, *1952*, I, 176.

86. See the statements by F. Kozhevnikov and J. Zourek which accepted the Fisheries Case as *lex ferenda*, pointing to the Svaerholthavet and Lopphavet basins as examples, *Yearbook of I.L.C.*, *1952*, I, 144, 189; objections by other members are on pp. 188-90.

87. *Yearbook of I.L.C.*, *1956*, I, 192; see also the statement by Jorge Castaneda, U.N. Gen. Ass., *Official Records*, 11th Sess., Sixth Committee (A/C.6/SR.496) (1956), p. 47.

88. Article 7(3), *A.J.I.L.*, L, 255-56.

89. *Yearbook of I.L.C.*, *1956*, I, 192-93, for the opposition by several states to the 25-mile limit.

90. Only M. O. Hudson "doubted that any definition of a bay existed in international law" as inferred from the Court's judgment in the Fisheries Case, *Yearbook of I.L.C.*, *1952*, I, 189.

91. Article 7(1), *A.J.I.L.*, L, 225; see I.C.J., *Pleadings*, I, 70, for exactly the same definition by Sir Eric Beckett.

tion that the Commission was prominently concerned with establishing a uniform rule in order to guide states objectively in the problems of delimitation, rather than leaving the whole concept of a bay to the subjective judgment of each state in accordance with the ambiguous position of the Court's judgment. On this point Iceland, objecting to the Commission's rejection of the judgment, declared that "the question of bays does not call for special rules" in the Fisheries Case.[92]

In the proceedings of the Geneva Conference in 1958 there was hardly any opposition to the final draft of the Commission so far as the definition of a bay in Article 7, paragraph 2, was concerned. The Conference debated, instead, on the maximum opening for a bay which would possess the character of internal waters, and finally accepted a proposal of twenty-four miles as a maximum for bay openings.[93]

At first glance, the outcome of the Conference, with its mechanical and mathematical formulae for bays, appears to be a total rejection of the far-reaching implications of the Fisheries Case. But the spirit of reasonable flexibility and local latitude is present in Article 7. For example, along an indented coast with a fringe of islands and where numerous mere curvatures exist, it would be difficult to decide whether the "general direction of the coast" rule (Article 4) or the twenty-four-mile rule (Article 7) should be resorted to.[94] In such a case, the coastal state seems to possess an option or latitude. In fact, the twenty-four-mile rule itself is a provision of flexibility and adaptability, since most bays, including historic bays, do not have larger openings.[95]

Historic bays had been considered a sort of "safety valve," providing flexibility in the law of the territorial sea,[96] for the protection of vital interests of coastal states. The Court in the Fisheries Case, favoring the Norwegian "vital bay" theory, set forth an "extremely liberal view"[97]

---

92. *A.J.I.L.*, L, 248.

93. Conference *Official Records*, III, 9, 21, 45, 145, for proposals for an identical maximum by Greece, Germany, Guatemala, and the U.S. The revised Soviet proposal in a joint amendment by Bulgaria, Poland, and the Soviet Union was accepted, 31 to 27 with 13 abstentions, in the First Committee (p. 145). Then it was adopted in plenary session, 63 to 6 with 5 abstentions (II, 63). See Article 7(4-5) in Appendix III below.

94. As pointed out by Denmark, Conference *Official Records*, III, 147; for an analysis of the flexible nature of delimitation of such bay or coast see Fitzmaurice, "Results of the Geneva Conference," pp. 80-81.

95. See McDougal and Burke, *Public Order*, p. 358, for the extent of many historic bays.

96. Gidel, *Droit international*, III, 651; Bourquin, *Baies historiques*, p. 38.

97. See Sir Gerald Fitzmaurice's comment to this effect, *Yearbook of I.L.C.*, *1955*, I, 178; cf. I.C.J., *Reports*, pp. 133, 138, 139, 142, 152, especially concerning the Svaerholthavet basin and historic titles.

by its overwhelming emphasis on Norway's geographical and economic conditions. In so doing, the Court almost destroyed the traditional concept of historic bays. Also noteworthy is the Soviet practice in claiming Peter the Great Bay as an historic bay, as previously discussed.

The work of the International Law Commission contained little by way of guidance on this problem. François, failing to treat historic bays in his first draft, left them "to be construed, in case of dispute, by the Court, *with due regard for all the features of the special case.*"[98] Thus in all drafts, historic bays were exempted from the provision for bays in general.

At the Geneva Conference of 1958 there was a general consensus among the delegations that there was no generally accepted rule for historic bays.[99] Eventually, a joint revised resolution submitted by India and Panama was accepted. It recommended that the General Assembly of the United Nations "arrange for the study" of the juridical status of historic bays and waters.[100]

It is difficult, indeed, to assess correctly how much influence the Fisheries Case exerted upon the Conference's decision on historic bays. But the flexibility left intact in the Court's concept of historic titles was certainly reflected in François' statement that the problem must be handled "with due regard for all the features of the special case." Thus, as the Court stated, "history together with other factors"[101] must be the basis for historic claim to certain bays, and such bays still remain as a sort of safety valve.

Seaward Jurisdictions.—A great number of states had enacted legislation expanding the breadth of their territorial seas since the Hague Conference of 1930, and, as one authority noted, "none of them had adhered to the three-mile limit."[102] Above all, the Court in the Fisheries Case appeared to have "delivered the *coup de grâce* to the three-mile rule as of absolute world-wide application,"[103] particularly in its general rejection of historic attitudes of the great maritime powers.

François attempted to modify this uncertain and fluid status of the territorial sea's breadth. He undoubtedly understood the danger of Alvarez' opinion, which left each state to decide the limit of its territorial

98. Conference *Official Records*, III, 69, italics added; see also *Yearbook of I.L.C., 1955*, I, 201-2, 211.
99. See statements to this effect by Sir Reginald Manningham-Buller and Peter H. Pfeiffer, Conference *Official Records*, III, 9, 45.
100. Conference *Official Records*, II, 68, III, 198, 252; Appendix III, below.
101. I.C.J., *Reports*, p. 133.
102. M. O. Hudson's statement, *Yearbook of I.L.C., 1952*, I, 166.
103. Allen, "Fishery Geography," p. 560.

sea upon its own criteria of reasonableness. In his first report he proposed a six-mile rule as a compromise—to find a new medium between national interests (the territorial sea) and the international aspect (the freedom of the seas).[104] Later, however, in recognition of the fact that some of the vital interests of a coastal state, specifically fishery interests, could not be satisfied by a narrow limit of the territorial sea,[105] François submitted an elaborate proposal. The territorial sea, according to it, would remain at three miles, but beyond this limit there could be nine more miles of a contiguous zone for fishery purposes.[106]

The reception of this report was divided in the Commission. On one hand, Lauterpacht, although conceding that the Fisheries Case recognized a certain amount of latitude for the coastal state, did not agree that "under existing law any State was free to fix at will, with an effect binding upon other States, the breadth of its territorial sea, in excess of the traditional limit." On the other hand, Georges Scelle asserted that "no rule of international law existed fixing the breadth of the territorial sea." Hudson suggested that the Fisheries Case provided "a number of useful pointers" in its general principles and criteria for the progressive development of international law.[107]

The attitudes of states on the problem were equally divided. One group, treating the implications of the Fisheries Case in a rather conservative manner, emphasized the "international aspect" of delimitation questions. According to this group, the freedom of the seas was considered to be "a universal and fundamental rule," from which the sovereignty of the coastal state over the territorial sea was a necessary "derogation" which must be kept to a minimum.[108] The other group of states resorted to a liberal interpretation. Accepting the latter view, Norway, using the Court's judgment, argued that: "It is the land which confers upon the coastal States a right to the waters off its coasts," and therefore "a State must be allowed the latitude necessary in order to be able to adapt its delimitation to practical needs and local requirements"[109]

104. See his explanation for the 6-mile rule, *Yearbook of I.L.C.*, *1952*, II, 31-32.
105. See especially a comment by Hudson that the maximum breadth could not be settled without providing an answer for the "question of all off-shore zones," *Yearbook of I.L.C.*, *1952*, I, 166.
106. See Agenda 53, p. 6, for his second and third reports; the latter made no substantive change in this respect.
107. *Yearbook of I.L.C.*, *1952*, I, 195, 158, 166; see also, pp. 159, 162, the denial of any uniform rule by Ricardo J. Alfaro and J. M. Yepes.
108. The Netherlands' statement, *A.J.I.L.*, L, 258; see pp. 274, 277 for the opinions of the U.S. and Great Britain in not such a direct manner.
109. *Yearbook of I.L.C.*, *1956*, II, 68-69; see pp. 70, 100 for similar statements by M. Lachs (Poland) and the Yugoslav government; cf. I.C.J., *Reports*, p. 133.

of the land in question. Israel agreed, pointing out the "essentially economic and sociological character" of the law of the territorial sea. Israel asserted that the Court had laid down that the law must take into account economic, social, and political factors, within "a general criterion of reasonableness" and that "what is reasonable in a given case depends upon all the circumstances."[110] This group thus excluded the consideration of historic titles rather in accord with Alvarez' opinion.

Consequently, the Commission in its report to the General Assembly concluded that "it is an incontrovertible fact that international practice is not uniform as regards the delimitation of the territorial sea," and yet that "international law does not permit an extension of the territorial sea beyond twelve miles"[111] as shown in the practices of a majority of states. It is of interest to note, however, that the Commission recommended that the extent of the territorial sea should be determined with regard for "economic and geographical factors." The General Assembly in its resolution calling for an international conference on the law of the seas followed this recommendation. It stated that the law should be examined in the light "not only of the legal but also of the technical, biological, economical and political aspects of the problems,"[112] in effect rejecting the inflexible attitudes of the great maritime powers in the past.

In the Geneva Conference of 1958, the principles and spirit underlying the Fisheries Case played very crucial roles. Those states which originally supported narrower limits of the territorial sea in favor of wider scope for the freedom of the seas frequently quoted two passages from the Court's opinion: "The delimitation of sea areas has always an international aspect: It cannot be dependent merely upon the will of the coastal States"; there should be a "more or less close relationship existing between certain [sea] areas and the land formation."[113] On the other hand, those states, particularly Afro-Asian, Latin American, and Communist countries, which had advocated wider limits and more flexi-

110. "Comments by Certain Governments," p. 1004; other opinions: *Yearbook of I.L.C.*, *1956*, II, 45, for Denmark; I, 171-72, for L. Padilla-Nervo (Mexico); U.N. Gen. Ass., *Official Records*, 11th Sess., Sixth Committee, pp. 69, 85, for Hans G. Anderson (Iceland) and Luis Melo Lacaros (Chile).

111. *Yearbook of I.L.C.*, *1956*, II, 265-66; see also *A.J.I.L.*, L, 222.

112. François' statement in U.N. Gen. Ass., *Official Records*, 11th Sess., Sixth Committee, p. 26; Resolution 1105 (XI) as adopted February 21, 1956, *ibid.*, Supplement No. 17 (A/3572).

113. Quoted from François' statement, Conference *Official Records*, III, 19; see pp. 11-12, 19, 24, for statements by Sweden, the Netherlands, Portugal, Japan, and the U.S.; for a more elaborate analysis see McDougal and Burke, *Public Order*, pp. 536-37, 554-57.

bility in determining the territorial sea resorted to the general criteria of the Court's judgment—"geographical realities," "economic interests, peculiar to certain regions," "practical needs and local requirements"[114] —and to the liberal spirit of the Court which was so strongly reinforced by Alvarez' opinion. This is well illustrated in the position taken by F. V. Garcia Amador who, acknowledging "a continuous process of transformation, the causes of which were often wholly outside the field of juridical science," asserted the need for "recognition of the special interests of the coastal States in the resources of the waters adjacent to their coasts" examined "in their proper perspective and interpreted in a manner consistent with reality."[115] Some states even asserted the priority of the territorial sea to the freedom of the seas. For example, Vladimir M. Koretsky, a Ukrainian delegate, argued at the 1960 Geneva Conference that it was not the principle of freedom of the seas which determined the extent of the territorial sea; rather it was "the extent of the high seas and the limit of the freedom of the sea which were determined by the limit of the territorial sea."[116] An exaggerated interpretation of Alvarez' opinion may be tantamount to this extreme assertion.

In attempts to strike a workable balance between the two groups of states, it was felt necessary to allow a rather wide extent of the territorial sea with a reasonable degree of flexibility. It was also considered necessary to take into account the most prominent "special interests" of the coastal states, in particular fishery interests.[117] In this spirit of moderation and conciliation the United States proposed that the maximum breadth of the territorial sea be set at six miles, with an additional six-mile zone for fishery rights, provided that the historic rights of other states (those existing for at least five years prior to the signing of the proposed convention) be guaranteed in the outer six-mile zone. Canada proposed the same limits, but made no provision for historic rights. India and Mexico jointly proposed that each state be allowed to set its own territorial sea up to a maximum of twelve miles; Yugoslavia made a similar proposal. The Soviet Union suggested that each state fix the boundaries of its territorial sea in accordance with established practice within the limits, *as a rule*, of three to twelve miles, having regard for historical and geographical conditions and economic and security interests.[118]

114. Statements by Argentina and Tunisia, Conference *Official Records*, III, 42, 45.
115. *Ibid.*, p. 233.
116. Second Conference *Official Records, Summary*, p. 116.
117. Statement by Max Sorensen, *ibid.*, p. 5.
118. Conference *Official Records*, Annex, p. 232-33, 248, 253-54.

But no proposal received the necessary majority vote in the plenary session, although the proposal of the United States came closest to being accepted.[119] Despite this failure, the Geneva Conference of 1958 made important progress with regard to other seaward jurisdictions. First, an agreement was reached on the right of a coastal state to establish contiguous zones for the purposes of preventing "infringement of its customs, fiscal, immigration or sanitary regulations within its territory or territorial sea" and for "punishing such infringements," though within a "decidedly anachronistic" limit of twelve miles from the coast.[120] It is significant to note, however, that "security" was excluded from the above provision, apparently leaving a great deal of latitude for the coastal states in deciding to go beyond the twelve-mile limit if necessary for defense or other national security purposes.[121]

Second, there was recognition of the "special rights" of a coastal state "in the maintenance of the productivity of the living resources in any area of the high seas adjacent to its territorial sea" and thus its right to "adopt unilateral measures of conservation" if "negotiations to that effect with other States concerned have not led to an agreement within six months."[122] This was in effect a recognition of the Latin American practice of fishery conservation over the vast continental seas, provided negotiations with other states had at least been attempted. Finally, the rights of the coastal state over the continental shelf were acknowledged. Although the legal status of the superjacent waters as high seas was not affected by this, the coastal states were given the right to construct 500-

119. Conference *Official Records*, II, 125.

120. Article 24, Appendix III, below; McDougal and Burke, *Public Order*, pp. 605, 607. Arthur Dean, "Geneva Conference," pp. 607, 624, interprets the article liberally: The coastal state might "adopt laws *prohibiting* activity in the contiguous zone the effect of which involved an infringement of the cited interests within the territorial sea or the territory of the state." For a more flexible interpretation see Oda, "Contiguous Zone," pp. 131-32.

121. It is indeed doubtful that nation-states would accept any legal limit for the protection of their "vital" interests, especially security. For example, the air defense line and atomic bomb testing over the high seas have been permitted strictly in violation of freedom of the air and sea. See the U.S. Security Control Air Defense Identification Zones, 14 C.F.R., §§ 620-12 (1-2) (1960 Supp.); also the atomic testing and its danger zone regulations, 33 C.F.R., §§ 204.1-204.235 (1961 Supp.). For the best defense of security zones see McDougal and Schlei, "Hydrogen Bomb Tests," pp. 674-82, 684-88. Because of the adamant attitude of the Western powers toward bomb testing on the open seas, a resolution proposed by India was adopted at the Geneva Conference of 1958, to defer any decision on whether such tests are "an infringement of the freedom of the seas"—Conference *Official Records*, II, 22-24, 98-99, 143.

122. Articles 6 and 7 of the Convention on Fishery and Conservation of the Living Resources of the High Seas, Conference *Official Records*, II, 139-40.

meter safety zones around installations and devices used in the exploration and exploitation of the shelf.[123]

In the Fisheries Case the Court had stated that "it is the land which confers upon the coastal state a right to the waters off its coasts." The Geneva Conference of 1958 gave full recognition to this principle and applied it in a manner consistent with reality, with thorough awareness of rapidly changing world conditions.

Against the background of these accomplishments, the Second Geneva Conference was called in March, 1960, to deal specifically with the problems of the territorial sea and the contiguous fishery zone. One thing was clear from the beginning: The majority of states favored a twelve-mile limit, either for the breadth of the territorial sea or for the territorial sea combined with a contiguous fishery zone. Only two proposals were seriously debated. The eighteen-power proposal,[124] sponsored by a combination of Asian, African, and Arab states and by Mexico and Venezuela, provided for a flexible limit of up to twelve miles for the territorial sea. If the state chooses a breadth less than twelve miles, it would be entitled to an additional twelve-mile exclusive fishery zone. The proposal also embodied a principle of reciprocity, according to which a state with a territorial sea or fishing zone less than twelve miles had "the right vis-à-vis any other State with a different delimitation thereof, to exercise the same sovereignty or exclusive fishing rights beyond its fixed limits up to the limits fixed by that other State."[125] This proposal was defeated by a close vote.

More nearly successful was the second proposal, a joint text of the United States and Canada. It proposed a six-mile territorial sea coupled with a six-mile contiguous fishing zone, subject to the right to continued fishing in the outer six miles for any state whose vessels had made a practice of fishing in such zone for a five-year period preceding January 1, 1958. But the right of continued fishing was to end after a period of ten years from October 31, 1960. Any disputes arising out of these provisions were to be submitted to a special international commission for settlement. This proposal failed to achieve the necessary two-thirds majority by a margin of but one negative vote. The important factor for this near success, however, was the acceptance of an amendment in

123. Articles 3 and 5, paragraphs 2 and 3, of the Convention on the Continental Shelf, *ibid.*, p. 142.

124. Ethiopia, Ghana, Guinea, Indonesia, Iran, Iraq, Jordan, Lebanon, Libya, Morocco, the Philippines, Saudi Arabia, Sudan, Tunisia, U.A.R., Yemen, Mexico, and Venezuela; the Soviet Union, withdrawing its own, joined the 18-power proposal later.

125. Second Conference *Official Records, Summary*, pp. 147, 165-66, 168.

the joint proposal which recognized "preferential fishing rights" of the coastal state beyond the territorial and fishery limits when certain special conditions existed and could be established before an impartial commission.[126]

The Conference's failure meant that there was still no hard and fast, generally agreed-upon rule on the extent of the territorial sea. Even though the general principles of the Fisheries Case were not, in this instance, formulated into workable rules, it is clear that the Geneva Conferences were much influenced by the Court's decision. This can be seen above all in the fact that the whole issue of seaward jurisdiction was examined not as a purely juridical problem which could be formulated into mechanical and rigid rules but as a problem with many dynamic facets—geographical, economic, social, and political. In this is clearly evident the influence of the liberal criteria and spirit of the Fisheries Case decision, frequently identified with Judge Alvarez' concurring opinion.

126. *Ibid.*, pp. 30, 166, 167, 190. The amendment was sponsored by Brazil, Cuba, and Uruguay. The vote on the proposal was 54 in favor, 28 against, and 5 abstentions; for an analysis see Dean, "Second Geneva Conference," pp. 751, 779-81.

5. CONCLUSION AND SEQUEL

The axiomatic principles of the international law of the sea developed since the time of Grotius are the freedom of the high seas and the territorial sea. Neither principle, however, has been considered absolute; the relative weight given to each at any particular time has depended upon the balance of divergent national interests. In this sense, as one authority points out, "It is an over-simplification to state that the problem . . . [is a] conflict between wider community interests [freedom of the seas] and narrow national self-interests [territorial sea]." The transformation of national interests, the pattern of political power, and the "political culture of the main actors" have always affected the relationship between the freedom of the seas and the territorial sea in the evolutionary development of the law of the sea.[1]

Two perennial problems born of this fluid relationship have been the extent of the seaward jurisdictions of the coastal state and the method of its delimitation. In the seventeenth and eighteenth centuries a few great maritime powers dominated the high seas and succeeded in monopolizing fisheries and navigation. They naturally preferred a narrow territorial sea and imposed upon many coastal states a minimal three-mile limit. But this balance of national interests was found increasingly inadequate for the maintenance of the well-being of nations during the late nineteenth century and particularly after the turn of the century. Many states expanded their territorial seas. Many others resorted to the contiguous zone, whose purposes ranged from neutrality, defense, smuggling, and customs enforcement to sanitary regulations and fishery conservation. More recently still others began to claim the continental shelf and even its superjacent waters for submerged mineral resources and for fishery conservation. These trends tended to make the expression "freedom of the high seas" meaningless or "a purely negative, worn-out concept."[2]

No less uncertain and transformed have been the problems of delimitation of the territorial sea. All the traditional concepts of the territorial sea which once enjoyed pre-eminence have been increasingly challenged: the low-water-mark rule or the coastal-baseline method; the ten-

1. Sorensen, "Law of the Sea," p. 190; Stanley Hoffman, "International Systems and International Law," in Knorr and Verba, *International System*, p. 211; see also Corbett, *Law in Diplomacy*, Chaps. 1-3.
2. U.N. Gen. Ass., *Memorandum on the Regime of the High Seas by G. Gidel*, pp. 2-3.

mile rule for the extent of straight baselines across a bay, between islands, and between islands and the mainland; and the concept of historic bays.

These developing trends have resulted in part from the impact on international law of international conferences, such as the Hague Conference of 1930; in part from the influence of new and newly influential members of the international community on development of the law and modification of the existing law; in part from the need to adapt the law to changed economic, social, and technological conditions; in part from the emergence of new problems with which international law is being called upon to concern itself for the first time. Few of the traditional topics of international law have escaped the influence of far-reaching changes, which in turn have left the law in a particularly fluid stage of development. As a result, the controversy over acceptable rules has raged unabated.

The Anglo-Norwegian fisheries dispute reflected all of this background of the law of the territorial sea. Great Britain, representing the historic attitudes of the traditionally powerful maritime states, asserted in effect the freedom of the seas as the fundamental precept to which all other aspects of the sea must conform. It argued that the three-mile rule for the extent of the territorial sea, the ten-mile rule for bays and islands, the low-water-mark rule for the normal baseline, and historic or prescriptive title for exceptional cases, were the rules which had been long established as the general rules of international law. On the other hand, Norway, more in the spirit of recent trends, averred that there had been no such hard and fast rules for the extent and delimitation of the territorial sea. Norway emphasized changing needs and requirements which should be reflected in the law of the sea. Pointing out that customary law by its very nature provides for reasonableness and adaptability, Norway claimed that the "general direction of the coast" rule should be the general rule.

In confronting these diametrically opposed views as to the delimitation of the territorial sea, which involved a dispute over the fundamental nature of the law itself, the International Court delivered a judgment with a threefold significance. First, the Court dealt with the Norwegian method of delimitation which Great Britain had challenged. The Court gave a short but clear judgment in favor of Norway and its straight-baseline system as applied by the Norwegian Royal Decree of 1935. The Court, accepting the "general direction of the coast" as a general rule of international law, maintained the position that "such general rules as there are possess a considerable degree of flexibility." On this basis, the Court decided against the ten-mile rule for the maximum opening of bays and for the distance between islands as an established rule of international law.

Second, the Court went beyond the particular questions in the dispute and dealt with the fundamental disagreement over the general principles and nature of the territorial sea. Throughout its judgment, the Court was consistent and invariable on the following principles relating to the law of the sea: (1) the "general direction of the coast" as a general rule for delimiting *any aspect* of the territorial sea, applicable to any specific case; (2) subjective and flexible criteria: the geographical realities, a "sufficiently closely linked" relationship between the land domain and the sea areas in question, and "certain economic interests peculiar to a region"; (3) historic factors, such as long usage and acquiescence by other states within a reasonable period of time, considered in conjunction with the prevailing economic and geographic factors; (4) applying general international law to specific cases "within the bounds of what is reasonable and moderate."

Third, the Court acknowledged, by the spirit if not by the letter of its decision, that the general rules concerning seaward jurisdictions ought to be examined by taking into consideration concrete expressions of the coastal state's legitimate interests, and thus refused to accept the historic attitudes of the traditional maritime powers on the allegedly settled rules of international law. This was in effect an authoritative endorsement of modern trends toward transformation of the law which had long preceded the Court's judgment.

Even more significance was added to these decisions by Judge Alvarez' concurring opinion, by far the most prominent in terms of subsequent developments in the law of the sea. Although it went beyond the scope of the Court's judgment in totally discarding any concept of historic factors, its merit lies in its succinct exposition of the legitimate-interest theory. Undoubtedly it was this aspect of Alvarez' opinion that was taken as sharing a common spirit with the Court's majority judgment, particularly in comparison with the history-minded dissenting opinions of McNair, Read, and Hsu Mo.

The Court's judgment was quickly followed by further expansion of the extent of the territorial sea and other seaward jurisdictions. Several states interpreted the judgment as a general sanction for change in traditional rules of the law of the sea. Iceland thus enforced not only the straight-baseline system along its entire coast, but extended its territorial sea to four miles in 1952 and its contiguous fishery zone to twelve miles in 1958, despite vigorous protest from Great Britain. The Latin

67

American states justified their claims to expanded jurisdiction over the superjacent waters of the continental shelf by asserting the nonexistence of any uniform rule as to maximum extent of the territorial sea and by interpreting liberally the flexible criteria of the Fisheries Case and those more forcibly set forth by Alvarez in his separate opinion. Since 1951 more than twenty states followed suit in expanding their territorial seas and other seaward jurisdictions. Particularly notable in this respect is the expansionist sentiment among the emerging nations of Africa, Asia, and Latin America. Indonesia implemented, as did the Philippines, the straight-baseline system in such a manner as to connect its thousands of islands, large or small, encompassing vast seas and straits. Finally, the Soviet Union claimed Peter the Great Bay as a historic bay, actually minimizing the historic title as had the Court in its judgment and stressing "vital bay" criteria. These trends certainly signified a general assault launched by many coastal states upon the principle of freedom of the seas in favor of the expansion of the territorial sea and of other seaward jurisdictions.

The International Law Commission, deliberating on this impact of the Fisheries Case and particularly Alvarez' opinion upon the practices of states, considered the Court's decision to be faulty primarily in its failure to provide an objective set of uniform standards and workable rules. The Commission, however, accepted the decision as *lex ferenda* and set out to rectify the status of the law of the sea in the light both of its general principles and of actual state practices. The Commission without doubt considered it an urgent task to save general objective rules of international law in the face of the described assault. The Commission's work thus reflected in general the conservative attitude based on the traditional concepts of international law, but still incorporated some outstanding contributions made by the Court in the Fisheries Case. The United Nations Conference met twice on the law of the sea (1958 and 1960 in Geneva) to codify the law in terms of the work of the Commission. It must be remembered that almost half of the membership of the Conference was composed of the small and newly emerging nations who were eager to take part in open forum and express their recently won independence. In this respect, and in terms of their general inclination to regard the traditional rules of international law as manifestations of colonialism, the liberal spirit of the Court's judgment and specifically of Alvarez' independent-minded opinion played a very conspicuous role. In this process of "progressive" development and codification of the law of the sea, the following rules were accepted:

First, although the low-water-mark rule was retained as a normal or general rule in delimitation of the territorial sea, the flexible use of the straight-baseline system was approved for "deeply indented" areas or areas with "a fringe of islands along the coast," with criteria almost identical with those set forth in the Fisheries Case. Moreover, no maximum was set for the length of a baseline. One important departure from the Court's judgment was the decision that economic interests could not justify the application of the straight-baseline system where the geographical conditions are not satisfied.

Second, use of a straight baseline for a coastal archipelago, which had direct sanction in the Court's judgment, was accepted as coming within a "special case" of the straight-baseline system—in connecting "appropriate points." Because of the complex problems of size, formation, and location, however, a rule for the oceanic archipelago was not seriously deliberated. In contrast with the Court's attitude toward drying rocks and shoals, which did not at all distinguish them from the definition of islands in selecting base points, the Commission and the 1958 Conference both rejected drying rocks and shoals as points of departure for the drawing of baselines.

Third, undoubtedly because of the Court's emphatic denial of the ten-mile rule for bays, the maximum permissible length of a straight baseline across a bay was set at twenty-four miles, a distance large enough to provide considerable flexibility. Furthermore, the question of historic bays, whether based on the vital-bay concept or on historic title, was left unsolved, partly because of the lack of information. The historic-bay argument remains as an important "safety valve," as Gilbert Gidel put it, in moderating conflicts over the territorial sea. The mechanical definition of a bay accepted by the Conference constitutes a significant deviation from the Court's opinion. The Court had practically destroyed any concept of a bay by including "minor curvatures" within the applicability of straight baselines.

Finally, the generally liberal spirit of the Court's opinion and particularly that of Judge Alvarez concerning the extent of the seaward jurisdiction played a prominent role in destroying any basis for discussion of the three-mile limit as a general rule. Although no decision was actually reached, the 1960 Conference came very close indeed to accepting a six-mile territorial sea with a further six-mile contiguous zone for fishing purposes.

Despite the failure of the Geneva Conferences to reach an agreement on a uniform extent of the territorial sea, the expanded economic interests of the coastal states were clearly recognized. This was evident both in the acceptance of the continental-shelf doctrine with a 500-meter safety or contiguous zone around any installation for exploitation of the resources of the sea, and in the recognition of the coastal states' "special interests" in fishery conservation on the high seas contiguous to their coasts, with the right of unilateral conservation measures in certain circumstances. Moreover, an important agreement was reached on the right of the coastal states to establish contiguous zones for customs, fiscal, immigration, or sanitary regulations, up to twelve miles from the coast. The omission of "security" purposes from the provision, if interpreted in a liberal spirit, may suggest an important reservation to the states of the right to extend the contiguous zone beyond the twelve-mile limit.

In the final analysis, the significance of the Fisheries Case has transcended the mere technicalities of delimitation contested between Great Britain and Norway. The Court's view that seaward jurisdiction is based upon accepted norms, geographic factors and state interests beyond purely historic factors, limited only by the requirements of reasonableness and flexibility, has had a great influence in the development of a modern international law of the sea. In its contention that the law was not merely juridical, the Court created a "daring piece of judicial legislation," as H. Lauterpacht states. Also noteworthy is the role played by Alvarez' concurring opinion as it was accepted by the small and emerging nations as justifying their cause of rebelling against the hitherto rigid attitude of maritime powers who emphasized the time-honored freedom of the seas and the narrow extent of the territorial sea and delimitation.

The failure to achieve agreement on a uniform extent of the territorial sea is not as serious as might appear. The problem is a complex one and any attempt to arbitrarily impose a technical and uniform rule simply for the sake of uniformity might well mean to place the law in an "unsuitable strait-jacket."[3] The criterion of general adaptability "within the bounds of what is reasonable and moderate," as maintained by the Court, would be a more appropriate principle for a law which is in a state of continuous transformation and whose sources of change are wholly outside the field of juridical science.

A reasonable and equitable approach to the problem of the extent of the territorial sea and other seaward jurisdictions has been demonstrated recently by Great Britain, which for so long adamantly opposed any

3. Quoted from Hale's warning to the Hague Codification Conference of 1930, in "Territorial Waters," p. 68. But there are writers who favor a world-wide agreement on a definite limit; on a 12-mile limit for all purposes, see Svarlien, "Territorial Sea," p. 351; on a 6-mile territorial sea and a further 6 miles for fishing, see McDougal and Burke, *Public Order*, pp. 519-20.

expansion of the seaward jurisdiction. Between the two Geneva Conferences on the Law of the Sea, Great Britain and Denmark reached an agreement on the expansion of the fishery zone of the Faroe Islands to six miles, pending the expected results of the second Conference in 1960.[4]

Shortly after that Conference ended, Great Britain went a step further. It indicated willingness to negotiate conventions by means of bilateral talks, along the lines of the United States-Canadian compromise proposal at the Conference (the six-mile territorial sea and a further six-mile contiguous zone for fisheries). Following Norway's extension of its territorial sea from four to six miles, Great Britain quickly approached Norway and agreed on November 17, 1960, not to object to exclusion of its fishing vessels from this six-mile territorial sea. The agreement also provided that, after October 31, 1970, Great Britain would not object to exclusion from a twelve-mile fishery zone which Norway was contemplating.[5] Similarly, in the Anglo-Icelandic Agreement of March 11, 1961, Great Britain finally agreed not to object to Iceland's twelve-mile fishing zone, provided that British vessels be permitted to fish within the outer six miles of the zone for three years. Significantly, the British government recognized "the exceptional dependence of the Icelandic nationals upon coastal fisheries for their livelihood and economic development."[6] In view of the above developments in extending the fishery zones to twelve miles, the Danish government announced that it considered the Anglo-Danish agreement of April, 1959, null and void. The Faroe government quickly established a twelve-mile fishery zone, effective March 24, 1964.[7] On April 29, 1963, the British government announced its final withdrawal from the worn-out North Sea Fisheries Treaty of 1882, which had established a three-mile limit for the territorial sea, and invited members of the European Free Trade Association, the European Economic Community, Iceland, the Irish Republic, and Spain to hold a conference on the fisheries problems.[8]

4. See Order No. 130 of April 27, 1959, in *United Nations Legislative Series, Supplement to the Laws and Regulations on the Regime of the Territorial Sea,* 1960; Great Britain, *Treaty Series,* No. 59.
5. *Times* (London), May 13, 1960; *New York Times,* May 14, 1960; Johnson, "Law of the Sea," pp. 590-91. The 12-mile zone became effective September 1, 1961, *New York Times,* March 21, 1961.
6. Johnson, "Law of the Sea," pp. 592-93; *New York Times,* March 10, 1961.
7. *Christian Science Monitor,* May 2, 1963; see also *Times* (London), May 31, June 1, 8, 1961.
8. Treaty of May 6, 1882, signed by Belgium, Denmark, France, Germany, Great Britain, and the Netherlands, cited in *U.N.L.S., Laws and Regulations on the Regime of the Territorial Sea,* 1957, p. 695; *New York Times,* April 30, 1963.

The European Fisheries Conference was thus held in London from December 3, 1963, to March 2, 1964, with sixteen states and the Com: mission of the European Economic Community participating.[9] The Conference adopted a draft fisheries convention which closely resembled the United States-Canadian proposal at the Geneva Conference on the Law of the Sea in 1960. First, the coastal state would exercise "the exclusive right to fish and exclusive jurisdiction in matters of fisheries within the belt of six miles measured from the baseline of its territorial sea" (Article 2), and within a further zone between six and twelve miles the right to fish would be exercised only by the coastal state and by other contracting parties whose fishing vessels "habitually fished in that belt between 1st January, 1953 and 31st December, 1962" (Article 3). Second, the parties to the convention agreed to implement the provisions concerning the straight-baseline system and the bay closing line as adopted at the Geneva Conference of 1958. Finally, the most notable aspect of the draft treaty was Article 11 in which a principle of adaptability and "preferential treatment" was accepted so that "a coastal state may exclude particular areas from the full application" of the above fishery limit and regulations "in order to give preference to the local population if it is overwhelmingly dependent upon coastal fisheries," subject to the agreement of the other signatories and on a non-discriminatory basis.[10]

This positive and realistic attitude of Great Britain and other participating states—not so much in its abandonment of the three-mile limit as in its bilateral and regional approach to the problems of the territorial sea and fishery interests—is based on their understanding of the changes that have taken place in the balance of the divergent interests of the coastal states.[11] The impetus for Great Britain's re-evaluation of its stand came from the Court's opinion in the Fisheries Case and was inspired particularly by the subsequent developments in state practices. The Court's role in reversing the position of the great maritime powers,

9. *A.J.I.L.*, LVIII (1964), Off. Doc., 1068; participating were Austria, Belgium, Denmark, France, the Federal Republic of Germany, Iceland, Ireland, Italy, Luxemburg, the Netherlands, Norway, Portugal, Spain, Sweden, Switzerland, and Great Britain.

10. *Ibid.*, pp. 1071-72. The convention was not signed by Iceland, Norway, and Switzerland. It was intended for "unlimited duration" with a proviso for possible withdrawal after 20 years by giving 2 years' notice. See pp. 1073-74.

11. See another important departure from the 3-mile limit: Japan's readiness to make concession to a 12-mile fishing limit for Korea and to the straight-baseline system, as shown in the Japanese-Korean Fisheries Conference in July, 1963. Korea, however, did not accede to the concession. See "Compromise by the End of the Year," pp. 13, 18.

which had so long and so persistently defended the traditional approach to the law of the sea, provides dramatic evidence of the great significance of the Fisheries Case decision in the evolution of the customary law of the sea, an influence which has not yet exhausted all of its potential.

APPENDICES

THE HAGUE CODIFICATION CONFERENCE OF 1930 AND THE VIEWS OF STATES ON THE LIMIT OF THE TERRITORIAL SEA

COUNTRY	LIMIT	ALTERNATIVE
Australia	3 miles	
Belgium	3 miles with contiguous zone	
Brazil	6 miles	
Canada	3 miles	
Chile	3 miles with contiguous zone	6 miles
China	3 miles	
Colombia	6 miles	
Cuba	6 miles with contiguous zone	
Czechoslovakia	*abstained*	
Denmark	3 miles	
Egypt	3 miles with contiguous zone	
Estonia	3 miles with contiguous zone	
Finland	4 miles with contiguous zone	
France	3 miles with contiguous zone	
Germany	3 miles with contiguous zone	
Great Britain	3 miles	
Greece	3 miles	3 miles with contiguous zone
Iceland	4 miles	
India	3 miles	
Ireland	3 miles with contiguous zone	
Italy	6 miles	
Netherlands	3 miles with contiguous zone	
New Zealand	3 miles	
Norway	4 miles	4 miles with contiguous zone
Japan	3 miles	
Latvia	6 miles with contiguous zone	
Persia	6 miles with contiguous zone	
Poland	3 miles with contiguous zone	
Portugal	6 miles with contiguous zone	12 miles
Rumania	6 miles with contiguous zone	
South Africa	3 miles	
Spain	6 miles with contiguous zone	
Sweden	4 miles	
U.S.S.R.	*no definite limit*	
United States	3 miles	3 miles with contiguous zone
Uruguay	6 miles with contiguous zone	
Yugoslavia	6 miles with contiguous zone	

Source: "League of Nations," *A.J.I.L.*, XXIV (1930), Supp. Annex III, 253-57.

APPENDIX II

THE EXTENTS OF THE TERRITORIAL SEA, CONTIGUOUS ZONES, AND THE CONTINENTAL SHELF AS CLAIMED AND PRACTICED BY STATES IN 1963

A. TERRITORIAL SEA

3 MILES	4-6 MILES	7-12 MILES AND MORE
Argentina	Cambodia—5 (1957)[a]	Albania—10 (1952)
Australia	Ceylon—6 (1957)	Bulgaria—12 (1951)
Belgium	Colombia—6	Chile—50 km
Brazil	Finland—4[a]	China (Communist)—12 (1958)[d]
Canada	Greece—6	Ecuador—12 (1951)[a]
China (Nationalist)	India—6 (1958)	El Salvador—200[a]
Cuba	Israel—6 (1956)	Ethiopia—12 (1953)
Denmark	Italy—6	Guatemala—12
Dominican Republic	Morocco—6[b]	Iceland—12 (1958)[ab]
Malaysia	Norway—6 (1960)[ac]	Indonesia—12 (1957)[a]
France	Portugal—6	Iran—12 (1959)
Ireland[a]	Spain—6	Iraq—12 (1958)
Japan	Sweden—4[a]	Libya—12 (1954)
Jordan	Thailand—6 (1958)	Mexico—9
Liberia	Uruguay—6	Panama—12 (1958)
Netherlands	Yugoslavia—6	Poland—12 (1956)
Pakistan		Rumania—12 (1951)
Tunisia		Saudi Arabia—12 (1958)
Union of South Africa		Turkey—12 (1957)
United Kingdom		U.S.S.R.—12
United States		United Arab Rep.—12 (1958)
		Venezuela—12 (1956)[a]

Extent of the Territorial Sea not indicated:
Burma, Honduras[e], Korea, Lebanon, Laos, Nicaragua, Peru[a], Philippines[a]
Extent of the Territorial Sea "in accordance with international law":
Costa Rica[a], Federal Republic of Germany, Monaco, New Zealand

B. CONTINENTAL SHELF

SEABED AND SUBSOIL ONLY	SOVEREIGNTY OVER SUPERJACENT WATERS
Australia (1953)[f]	Argentina—limit unspecified (1946)
Brazil (1950)	Cambodia—to depth of 50 meters (1957)
Guatemala (1956)	Ceylon—100 miles from the territorial
Honduras (1957)[g]	sea (1957)
India (1955)	Chile—200 miles (1947)
Israel (1953)	Ecuador—to depth of 200 meters[i]
Malaysia[h]	El Salvador—200 miles (1950)
Pakistan (1950)	Iceland—limit unspecified (1948)
Philippines (1949)	Korea—limit unspecified (1952)
Portugal (1956)	Mexico—limit unspecified (1945)
Saudi Arabia (1949)	Nicaragua—limit unspecified (1950)
United States (1945)	Panama—limit unspecified (1946)
Venezuela (1956)	Peru—200 miles (1947)

C. Special Limits Claimed for Fishing and Other Purposes

Fishing	Customs, Security, and Other Zones
Argentina—10 miles	Argentina—12 miles (customs, security, sanitary regul.)
Australia—unspecified[f]	Belgium—10 km (customs)
Brazil—12 miles	Cambodia—12 miles (customs, security)
Cambodia—12 miles	Canada—12 miles (customs)
Canada—12 miles	Ceylon—6 miles (customs, criminal j'diction)
Ceylon—100 miles	Chile—100 km (customs, security)
Chile—200 miles	China (Nationalist)—12 miles (customs)
China (Communist)—unspecified[j]	Colombia—20 km (customs); 12 miles (sanitary regul.)
Colombia—12 miles	Cuba—12 miles (customs); 5 miles (sanitary regul.)
Costa Rica—200 miles	Denmark—4 miles (customs)
Dominican Rep.—15 miles	Dominican Rep.—15 miles (customs, security, sanitary regul.)
Denmark—12 miles (for Faroe Island)	Finland—6 miles (customs)
Ecuador—200 miles[i]	France—20 km (customs); 6 miles (security neutrality)
El Salvador—200 miles	Greece—10 miles (security)
Iceland—12 miles	Guatemala—12 miles (customs, neutrality)
India—100 miles	India—12 miles (customs, sanitary regul.)
Korea—20-200 miles	Italy—12 miles (customs); 10 miles (security)
Lebanon—6 miles	Japan—10 km (sanitary regul.)
Mexico—unspecified	Monaco—20 km (customs)
Morocco—6 miles	Norway—10 miles (customs)
Norway—12 miles	Saudi Arabia—18 miles (customs, security, sanitary regul.)
Panama—unspecified	United States—12 miles (customs)[k]
Peru—200 miles	United Kingdom—limit unspecified (customs)[l]
Portugal—reciprocity	Venezuela—15 miles (customs, security, sanitary regul.)
Thailand—12 miles	
Tunisia—to depth of 50 meters	
Venezuela—non-exclusive fishing limit over the continental sea	
Yugoslavia—10 miles	
U.S.S.R.—unspecified[m]	

a—Measured from straight baseline.
b—For fishing only.
c—As cited in *New York Times*, May 14, 1960.
d—As cited in *New York Times*, September 5, 1958.
e—Right to determine in future.
f—The Pearl Fisheries Act of 1952-1953 excludes other nationals from pearl fishing. See Oda, *The Structure of the International Law of the Sea*, pp. 80-81.
g—But see its 1951 decree claiming sovereignty over the continental sea.
h—The Federation of Malaysia came into existence in 1963 by incorporating North Borneo and Sarawak with Malaya and Singapore. Great Britain formerly declared its right over the seabed and subsoil of the continental shelf of North Borneo (1954) and Sarawak (1954).
i—Ecuador, by joining with Chile and Peru in the Declaration of Santiago on August 18, 1952, in effect claims its sovereignty over a 200-mile maritime zone.
j—The East China Sea and the Yellow Sea have been frequently claimed as part of China, in part based on the continental shelf doctrine. On April 15, 1955,

the Sino-Japanese Fisheries Treaty was concluded to allow Japan fishing right within certain restricted areas of the Sea. See Oda, *The Structure of the International Law of the Sea*, pp. 120-21.

k—The Anti-Smuggling Act of 1935 authorizes the President of the United States to declare a special limit of 50 miles beyond the customs enforcement zone (12 miles). Above pp. 10-11.

l—See the 1949 decision of *Attorney General* v. *Hunter*, (1949) 2 K.B. 111. Above p. 11, notes 41 and 42.

m—The decree of March 21, 1956 closed Tartarskie Strait and the whole of the Sea of Okhotsk (west of the Kuriles) for fishing by other nationals. Subsequently the Soviet-Japanese Fisheries Treaty of 1956 allowed the Japanese fishermen periodical right to fish in specified areas. See Oda, *The Structure of the International Law of the Sea*, pp. 81-82, 133-49.

Source: Mainly based on U.N. Synoptical Table (Doc. A/Conf.19/4), in Second United Nations Conference on the Law of the Sea, *Official Record, Summary Records of Plenary Meetings and Meetings of the Committee of the Whole* (A/Conf. 19/8) (1960).

APPENDIX III

CONVENTION ON THE TERRITORIAL SEA AND THE CONTIGUOUS ZONE ADOPTED BY THE UNITED NATIONS CONFERENCE ON THE LAW OF THE SEA IN 1958

ARTICLE 1

1. The sovereignty of a State extends, beyond its land territory and its internal waters, to a belt of sea adjacent to its coast, described as the territorial sea.

2. This sovereignty is exercised subject to the provisions of these articles and to other rules of international law.

ARTICLE 2

The sovereignty of a coastal State extends to the air space over the territorial sea as well as to its bed and subsoil.

ARTICLE 3

Except where otherwise provided in these articles, the normal baseline for measuring the breadth of the territorial sea is the low-water line along the coast as marked on large-scale charts officially recognized by the coastal State.

ARTICLE 4

1. In localities where the coastline is deeply indented and cut into, or if there is a fringe of islands along the coast in its immediate vicinity, the method of straight baselines joining appropriate points may be employed in drawing the baseline from which the breadth of the territorial sea is measured.

2. The drawing of such baselines must not depart to any appreciable extent from the general direction of the coast, and the sea areas lying within the lines must be sufficiently closely linked to the land domain to be subject to the regime of internal waters.

3. Baselines shall not be drawn to and from low-tide elevations, unless lighthouses or similar installations which are permanently above sea level have been built on them.

4. Where the method of straight baselines is applicable under the provisions of paragraph 1, account may be taken, in determining particular baselines, of economic interests peculiar to the region concerned, the reality and the importance of which are clearly evidenced by a long usage.

5. The system of straight baselines may not be applied by a State in such a manner as to cut off from the high seas the territorial sea of another State.

6. The coastal State must clearly indicate straight baselines on charts, to which due publicity must be given.

ARTICLE 5

1. Waters on the landward side of the baseline of the territorial sea form part of the internal waters of the State.

2. Where the establishment of a straight baseline in accordance with article 4 has the effect of enclosing as internal waters areas which previously had been considered as part of the territorial sea or of the high seas, a right of innocent passage, as provided in articles 14 to 23, shall exist in those waters.

ARTICLE 6

The outer limit of the territorial sea is the line every point of which is at a distance from the nearest point of the baseline equal to the breadth of the territorial sea.

ARTICLE 7

1. This article relates only to bays the coasts of which belong to a single State.

2. For the purposes of these articles, a bay is a well-marked indentation whose penetration is in such proportion to the width of its mouth as to contain landlocked waters and constitute more than a mere curvature of the coast. An indentation shall not, however, be regarded as a bay unless its area is as large as, or larger than, that of the semi-circle whose diameter is a line drawn across the mouth of that indentation.

3. For the purpose of measurement, the area of an indentation is that lying between the low-water mark around the shore of the indentation and a line joining the low-water mark of its natural entrance points. Where, because of the presence of islands, an indentation has more than one mouth, the semi-circle shall be drawn on a line as long as the sum total of the lengths of the lines across the different mouths. Islands within an indentation shall be included as if they were part of the water area of the indentation.

4. If the distance between the low-water marks of the natural entrance points of a bay does not exceed twenty-four miles, a closing line may be drawn between these two low-water marks, and the waters enclosed thereby shall be considered as internal waters.

5. While the distance between the low-water marks of the natural entrance points of a bay exceeds twenty-four miles, a straight baseline of twenty-four miles shall be drawn within the bay in such a manner as to enclose the maximum area of water that is possible with a line of that length.

6. The foregoing provisions shall not apply to so-called "historic" bays, or in any case where the straight baseline system provided for in article 4 is applied.

ARTICLE 10

1. An island is a naturally formed area of land, surrounded by water, which is above water at high tide.

2. The territorial sea of an island is measured in accordance with the provisions of these articles.

ARTICLE 11

1. A low-tide elevation is a naturally formed area of land which is surrounded by and above water at low-tide but submerged at high tide. Where a low-tide elevation is situated wholly or partly at a distance not exceeding the breadth of the territorial sea from the mainland or an island, the low-water line on that elevation may be used as the baseline for measuring the breadth of the territorial sea.

2. Where a low-tide elevation is wholly situated at a distance exceeding the breadth of the territorial sea from the mainland or an island, it has no territorial sea of its own.

ARTICLE 24

1. In a zone of the high seas contiguous to its territorial sea, the coastal State may exercise the control necessary to:

a) Prevent infringement of its customs, fiscal, immigration or sanitary regulations within its territory or territorial sea;

b) Punish infringement of the above regulations committed within its territory or territorial sea.

2. The contiguous zone may not extend beyond twelve miles from the baseline from which the breadth of the territorial sea is measured.

3. Where the coasts of two States are opposite or adjacent to each other, neither of the two States is entitled, failing agreement between them to the contrary, to extend its contiguous zone beyond the median line every point of which is equidistant from the nearest points on the baselines from which the breadth of the territorial seas of the two States is measured.

RESOLUTION VII ON REGIME OF HISTORIC WATERS

The United Nations Conference on the Law of the Sea,

Considering that the International Law Commission has not provided for the regime of historic waters, including historic bays,

Recognizing the importance of the juridical status of such areas,

Decides to request the General Assembly of the United Nations to arrange for the study of the juridical regime of historic waters, including historic bays, and for the communication of the results of such study to all States Members of the United Nations.

Source: U.N. Doc. A/Conf.13/L.52 and A/Con.13/L.56, adopted by the Conference at its 20th plenary meeting, as excerpted from U.N. Conference on the Law of the Sea, *Official Records*, Vol. II (A/Conf.13/38), Annexes, pp. 132-135, 145.

SELECTED BIBLIOGRAPHY

COURT REPORTS, STATUTES, TREATIES AND OTHER ACTS

California. *Government Code.* San Francisco: Bancroft-Whitney, 1951.
Great Britain. *The Statutes at Large.* 9 George II; 4, 42 George III; 4 George IV; 2-59 Victoria.
————. *Treaty Series.* London: His Majesty's Stationery Office, 1923, 1942, 1959. No. 16 (1923), No. 10 (1942), No. 59 (1959).
International Court of Justice. *Fisheries Case (United Kingdom v. Norway) Judgment of 18 December 1951: Reports of Judgments, Advisory Opinions and Orders.* Leyden: Sijthoff, 1951.
————. *Fisheries Case (United Kingdom v. Norway) Judgment of 18 December 1951: Pleadings, Oral Arguments, Documents.* 4 vols. Leyden: Sijthoff, 1951.
————. *Reports of Judgments, Advisory Opinions and Orders, 1949.* Leyden: Sijthoff, 1949.
League of Nations. *Treaty Series.* 205 vols. Geneva: Secretariat of the League of Nations, 1920-43. Vols. IX-XLII.
United Nations. *Legislative Series, Laws and Regulations on the Regime of the High Seas.* U.N. Doc. ST/LEG/SER.B/1. Lake Success, 1951.
————. *Legislative Series, Laws and Regulations on the Regime of the Territorial Sea.* U.N. Doc. ST/LEG/SER.B/6. Lake Success, 1957.
————. *Legislative Series, Supplement to the Laws and Regulations on the Regime of the Territorial Sea.* U.N. Doc. A/Conf. 19/5. Lake Success, 1960.
United States. *Federal Register.* Vol. X (1945). Washington: Government Printing Office, 1946.
————. *The Statutes at Large.* Vols. I-LXVII.
————. *United States Code.* Vol. XLIII (1953).
————. Supreme Court. *United States Reports,* 358 vols. Washington: United States Government Printing Office, 1798-1959. Vols. VI-CCXL.

STATE PAPERS AND OTHER DOCUMENTS

Great Britain. Foreign Office. *British and Foreign State Papers, 1812-.* 156 vols. London: His Majesty's Stationery Office, 1841-1959. Vols. I (1812)-CVII (1914).
————. Reference Division, Central Office of Information. *The Territorial Sea.* Classification I. le, N. R. 3790, January 1958. London: Her Majesty's Stationery Office, 1958.
Iceland. *The Icelandic Efforts for Fisheries Conservation, Memorandum Submitted to the Council of Europe by the Government of Iceland.* Reykjavik, September, 1954.
————. *The Icelandic Fisheries Limits.* Reykjavik: Edda Ltd., 1958.
————. *The Icelandic Fishery Question, Memorandum Submitted by the Government of Iceland to the General Assembly of the United Nations.* Reykjavik, September, 1958.
————. Ministry for Foreign Affairs. *British Aggression in Icelandic Waters.* Reykjavik, June, 1959.
League of Nations. *Acts of the Conference for the Codification of International Law, March 13-April 12, 1930, Vol. III: Minutes of the Second Committee, Territorial Waters.* C.351(b). M145(b). 1930.V. Geneva, 1930.
————. Committee of Experts for Progressive Codification of International Law. *Report of the Sub-Committee II, Questionnaire No. 2: Territorial Waters.* C.44.M.21.1926.V. Geneva, 1926.

81

League of Nations. Conference for Codification of International Law. *Bases of Discussion Drawn up for the Conference by the Preparatory Committee, Vol. II. Territorial Waters.* C.74.M.39.1929.V. Geneva, 1929.

United Nations. *Yearbook of the International Law Commission, 1952.* U.N. Doc. A/CN.4/Ser.A/1952, 2 vols. Lake Success, 1958.

————. *Yearbook of the International Law Commission, 1954.* U.N. Doc. A/CN.4/Ser.A/1954. Lake Success, 1959.

————. *Yearbook of the International Law Commission, 1955.* U.N. Doc. A/CN.4/Ser.A/1955. Lake Success, 1960.

————. *Yearbook of the International Law Commission, 1956.* U.N. Doc. A/CN.4/Ser.A/1956, 2 vols. Lake Success, 1956.

————. General Assembly. *Official Records.* Lake Success, 1952-1958.

————. General Assembly. *Report of the International Law Commission, Official Records.* 5th Sess., Supp. No. 12, A/1316. Lake Success, 1950.

————. General Assembly. *Report of the International Law Commission, Official Records.* 8th Sess., Supp. No. 9, A/2456. Lake Success, 1953.

————. General Assembly. *Report of the International Law Commission, Official Records.* 10th Sess., Supp. No. 9, A/2934. Lake Success, 1955.

————. General Assembly. *Report of the International Law Commission, Official Records.* 11th Sess., Supp. No. 9, A/3159. Lake Success, 1956.

————. General Assembly. *Memorandum on the Regime of the High Seas by G. Gidel.* A/CN.4/32, 14 July 1950. Lake Success, 1950.

————. General Assembly. *Report on the Regime of the Territorial Sea by J. P. A. François.* A/CN.4/53, 4 April 1952. Lake Success, 1952.

————. General Assembly. *Report on the Regime of the Territorial Sea by J. P. A. François.* A/CN.4/61, 19 February 1953. Lake Success, 1953.

————. Conference on the Law of the Sea. *Official Records.* 4 vols. A/Conf. 13/37-40. Lake Success, 1958.

————. Second Conference on the Law of the Sea. *Official Records, Summary Record of Plenary Meetings and Meetings of Committee of Whole.* A/Conf.19/8. Lake Success, 1960.

United States. *Congressional Records.* Vol. XCVIII.

————. Department of State. *Foreign Relations of the United States, Diplomatic Papers,* 1861-1946. Washington: Government Printing Office, 1861-1956.

————. North Atlantic Coast Fisheries Arbitration. *Proceedings before the Permanent Court of Arbitration at the Hague.* Senate Document No. 870. 61st Cong., 3d Sess. 12 Vols. Washington: Government Printing Office, 1912.

INTERNATIONAL LAW DIGESTS

Hackworth, G. H. *Digest of International Law.* 8 vols. Washington: Government Printing Office, 1940-1944.

Lauterpacht, H. (ed.). *Annual Digest and Reports of Public International Law Cases.* 1919-1922-1950. London: Butterworth, 1922-56.

Moore, John Bassett. *A Digest of International Law.* 8 vols. Washington: Government Printing Office, 1906.

COLLECTIONS OF CASES, TREATIES, DOCUMENTS, AND OTHER REPORTS

Bayitch, S.ʾ A. *Interamerican Law of Fisheries, an Introduction with Documents.* New York: Oceana Publications, 1957.

Briggs, Herbert W. (ed.). *The Law of Nations; Cases, Documents, Notes.* 2d ed. New York: Appleton, 1952.

Dowling, Noel T. *Cases of Constitutional Law.* 5th ed. New York: The Foundation, 1954.

Hudson, Manley O. *International Legislation, 1919-1945.* 9 vols. New York: Carnegie Endowment, 1931-50.

Marsden, R. G. *Documents Relating to Law and Custom of the Sea*. Vol. I. London: Navy Records Society, 1915-16.

Moore, John Bassett. *History and Digest of International Arbitrations to which the United States Has Been a Party*. 6 vols. Washington: Government Printing Office, 1898.

Scott, James Brown (ed.). *The Hague Court Reports*. New York: Oxford University, 1916.

Smith, H. A. *Great Britain and the Law of Nations; a Selection of Documents Illustrating the Views of the Government in the United Kingdom upon the Matters of International Law*. 2 vols. London: King, 1932-35.

GENERAL TREATISES ON INTERNATIONAL LAW

Brierly, James L. *The Law of Nations: An Introduction to the International Law of Peace*. 5th ed. Oxford: Clarendon, 1955.

Commission to Study the Organization of Peace. *Organizing Peace in the Nuclear Age*. New York, 1959.

Corbett, Percy C. *Law in Diplomacy*. Princeton: Princeton University, 1959.

Hall, William Edward. *International Law*. Oxford: Clarendon, 1880.

Hyde, Charles Cheney. *International Law, Chiefly as Interpreted and Applied by the United States*. 2 vols. 3d ed. Boston: Little, Brown, 1947.

Jenks, C. Wilfred. *The Common Law of Mankind*. New York: Praeger, 1958.

Kaplan, Morton A., and Nicholas deB. Katzenbach. *The Political Foundation of International Law*. New York: John Wiley, 1961.

Knorr, Klaus, and Sidney Verba (eds.). *The International System: Theoretical Essays*. Princeton: Princeton University, 1961.

Lauterpacht, H. *The Development of International Law by the International Courts*. New York: Praeger, 1958.

Martens, George Friedrich von. *Summary of the Law of Nations*. Trans. William Cobbett. Philadelphia: Thomas Bradford, 1795.

Oppenheim, L. *International Law, a Treatise*. 2 vols. 8th ed. H. Lauterpacht. London: Longmans, Green, 1955.

Röling, B. V. A. *International Law in an Expanded World*. Amsterdam: Djambaton, 1960.

Svarlien, Oscar. *An Introduction to the Law of Nations*. New York: McGraw Hill, 1955.

Westlake, John. *International Law*. Vol. I. 1st ed. Cambridge: University, 1904.

SPECIAL WORKS ON THE LAW OF THE SEA

Bartley, Ernest R. *The Tidelands Oil Controversy; a Legal and Historical Analysis*. Austin, Texas: University of Texas, 1953.

Bingham, Joseph W. *Report on the International Law of Pacific Coastal Fisheries*. Stanford: Stanford University, 1939.

Boggs, S. Whittemore. *International Boundaries—A Study of Boundary Functions and Problems*. New York: Columbia University, 1940.

Bourquin, Maurice. *Les baies historiques*. Geneva: Melanges Sauer Hall, 1952.

Bustemante y Sirvén, Antonio Sánchez de. *The Territorial Sea*. New York: Oxford University, 1930.

Bynkershoek, Cornellius van. *De dominio maris dissertatio*. Written in 1702, trans. Ralph Van Dewan Magoffin. New York: Carnegie Endowment, 1923.

Fenn, Percy Thomas, Jr. *The Origin of the Right of Fishery in Territorial Waters*. Cambridge, Mass.: Harvard University, 1926.

Fulton, Thomas W. *The Sovereignty of the Sea*. Edinburgh: Blackwood, 1911.

Garcia Amador, F. V. *The Exploitation and Conservation of the Resources of the Sea: A Study of the Resources of the Sea*. 2d ed. Leyden: Sythoff, 1959.

Gidel, Gilbert. *Le droit international public de la mer*. 3 vols. Châteauroux: Etablissements Mellottée, 1932-34.

Gidel, Gilbert. *Le plateau continental.* The Hague: Nijhoff, 1952.

Grotius, Hugo. *The Freedom of the Seas.* Trans. Ralph Van Dewan Magoffin, with revision of the Latin Text of 1633, ed. James B. Scott. New York: Oxford University, 1916.

Higgins, A. Pearce, and C. J. Colombos. *International Law of the Sea.* New York: Longmans, Green, 1945.

————. *International Law of the Sea.* 3d ed. London: Longmans, Green, 1954.

Jessup, Philip C. *The Law of Territorial Waters and Maritime Jurisdiction.* New York: Jennings, 1927.

Leonard, L. Larry. *International Regulations of Fisheries.* Washington: Carnegie Endowment, 1944.

McDougal, Myres S., and William T. Burke. *The Public Order of the Oceans: A Contemporary International Law of the Sea.* New Haven: Yale University, 1962.

Meyer, Christopher, B. V. *The Extent of Jurisdiction in Coastal Waters.* Leyden: Nijhoff, 1937.

Mouton, M. W. *The Continental Shelf.* The Hague: Nijhoff, 1952.

Oda, Shigeru. *The Structure of the International Law of the Sea* (Kaiyo no Kokusai-ho-Kozo). Tokyo: Yushindo, 1957.

Reinkemeyer, Hans-Albert, *Die sowjetische Zwölfmeilenzone in der Ostsee und die Freiheit des Meeres.* Heft 30, Beiträge zum Ausländischen Offentlichen Recht and Völkerrecht. Berlin: Carl Heymanns, 1955.

Riesenfeld, Stefan A. *Protection of Coastal Fisheries under International Law.* New York: Carnegie Endowment, 1942.

Smith, H. A. *The Law and Custom of the Sea.* 2d ed. London: Stevens, 1950.

Welwood, William. *An Abridgement of All Sea-Lawes.* London: H. Lownes, for T. Man, 1613. .

PERIODICAL ARTICLES

Allen, Edward W. "Fishery Geography of the North Pacific Ocean," *Geographical Review,* XLIII (1953), 557-62.

————. "Territorial Waters and Extraterritorial Rights," *American Journal of International Law,* XLVII (1953), 478-80.

Aramburú y Menchaca, Andrés A. "Character and Scope of the Rights Declared and Practiced over the Continental Shelf and Sea," *American Journal of International Law,* XLVII (1953), 120-23.

Balch, Thomas Willing. "Is Hudson Bay a Closed or an Open Sea?" *American Journal of International Law,* VI (1912), 409-59.

Barnes, Kathleen, and Homer E. Gregory. "Alaskan Salmons in World Politics," *Far Eastern Survey,* VII (1938), 47-53.

Bingham, Joseph W. "Juridical Status of the Continental Shelf," *Southern California Law Review,* XXVI (1952-1953), 4-20.

Boggs, S. Whittemore. "Delimitation of Seaward Areas under National Jurisdiction," *American Journal of International Law,* XLV (1951), 240-66.

————. "Delimitation of the Territorial Sea: The Method of Delimitation Proposed by the Delegation of the United States at the Hague Conference for the Codification of International Law," *American Journal of International Law,* XXIV (1930), 541-55.

————. "National Claims in Adjacent Seas," *Geographical Review,* XLI (1951), 185-209.

Brierly, James L. "The Doctrine of the Contiguous Zone and the Dicta in *Croft v. Dunphy,*" *British Yearbook of International Law,* XIV (1933), 155-57.

Brown, Philip Marshall. "Protective Jurisdiction," *American Journal of International Law,* XXXIV (1940), 112-16.

"Comments by Certain Governments on the Provisional Articles Covering the Regime of the High Seas and Draft Articles on the Regime of the Territorial

Sea, Adopted by the United Nations International Law Commission at Its Seventh Session in 1955," *American Journal of International Law*, L (1956), Off. Doc., 992-1049.

"Compromise by the End of the Year in the Japanese-Korean Conference? (Nennai Dakyo? Nikkan Kosho)," *Economist* (Ekonomisto), XLI, No. 32 (August 13, 1963), 13-18.

"Consultative Meeting of Foreign Ministers of the American Republics," *Department of State Bulletin*, I (1939), 321-37.

Cosford, Edwin J. "The Continental Shelf, 1910-1945," *The McGill Law Journal*, IV (1958), 245-66.

Dean, Arthur H. "The Geneva Conference on the Law of the Sea: What Was Accomplished," *American Journal of International Law*, LII (1958), 607-28.

—————. "Second Geneva Conference on the Law of the Sea; The Fight for Freedom of the Sea," *American Journal of International Law*, LIV (1960), 751-81.

De Visscher, Charles. "Reflections on the Present Prospects of International Adjudication," *American Journal of International Law*, L (1956), 467-74.

Evensen, Jens. "The Anglo-Norwegian Fisheries Case and Its Legal Consequences," *American Journal of International Law*, XLVI (1952), 603-30.

Fitzmaurice, Sir Gerald. "The Law and Procedure of the International Court of Justice, 1951-54: General Principles and Sources," *British Yearbook of International Law*, XXXI (1954), 27-70.

—————. "The Law and Procedure of the International Court of Justice, 1951-54: Points of Substantive Law, Part I: Maritime Law," *British Yearbook of International Law*, XXXI (1954), 371-429.

—————. "Some Results of the Geneva Conference on the Law of the Sea, Part I—The Territorial Sea and Contiguous Zone and Related Topics," *International and Comparative Law Quarterly*, VIII (1959), 73-123.

Green, L. C. "The Anglo-Norwegian Fisheries Case, 1951," *The Modern Law Review*, XV (1952), 373-77.

Hale, Richard W. "Territorial Waters as a Test of Codification," *American Journal of International Law*, XXIV (1930), 65-78.

"International Court Upholds Norway's Measurement of Territorial Sea from Baseline Drawn between Selected Points of Outlying Islands," *Harvard Law Review*, LXV (1952), 1453-56.

Iriye, Keishiro. "The Status of Peter the Great Bay (Piyotoru-Taitei-Wan no Chiyi)," *Legal Reports* (Horitsu Ziho), XXIX (1957), 1166-67.

Jessup, Philip C. "The Anti-Smuggling Act of 1935," *American Journal of International Law*, XXXI (1937), 101-6.

—————. "The Pacific Coast Fisheries," *American Journal of International Law*, XXXIII (1939), 124-38.

Johnson, D. H. N. "The Anglo-Norwegian Fisheries Case," *International and Comparative Law Quarterly*, I (1952), 145-80.

—————. "Icelandic Fishery's Limits," *International and Comparative Law Quarterly*, I (1952), 71-73, 350-54.

—————. "Law of the Sea: Development Since the Geneva Conference of 1958 and 1960: Anglo-Scandinavian Agreements Concerning the Territorial Sea and Fishing Limits," *International and Comparative Law Quarterly*, X (1961), 587-97.

Kent, H. S. K. "The Historical Origin of the Three-Mile Limit," *American Journal of International Law*, XLVIII (1954), 537-53.

Kuntz, Joseph L. "The Changing Law of Nations," *American Journal of International Law*, LI (1957), 77-83.

—————. "Continental Shelf and International Law; Confusion and Abuse," *American Journal of International Law*, L (1956), 828-53.

Lauterpacht, H. "Freedom of the Seas: Implications of the Norwegian Fisheries Case," *The Times* (London), January 8, 1952, p. 7.

————. "Sovereignty over Submarine Areas," *British Yearbook of International Law*, XXVII (1950), 376-433.

"League of Nations, Conference for the Codification of International Law, Held at the Hague, March-April, 1930," *American Journal of International Law*, XXIV (1930), Supp. 1-258.

McDougal, Myres S., and Nobert A. Schlei, "The Hydrogen Bomb Tests in Perspective: Lawful Measures for Security," *Yale Law Journal*, LXIV (1955), 648-710.

Nakamura, Takeshi. "The Significance of the Anglo-Norwegian Fisheries Case in International Law (Igirisu-Noruwei Gyogyo-Jiken no Kokusai-ho-teki Igi)," *Journal of International Law and Diplomacy* (Kokusaiho Gaiko Zasshi), LVI (1953), 250-80.

O'Connell, D. P. "The Geneva Conference on the Law of the Sea: Possible Implications for Australia," *The Australian Law Journal*, XXXII (1958-59), 134-37.

————. "Sedentary Fisheries and the Australian Continental Shelf," *American Journal of International Law*, XLIX (1955), 185-209.

Oda, Shigeru. "The Concept of the Contiguous Zone," *International and Comparative Law Quarterly*, XI (1962), 130-41.

Pakasi, C. R. "Indonesia and the Geneva Conference on the Law of the Sea," *The Indonesian Spectator*, II, No. 10 (April, 1958), 16-17.

Reeves, Jesse S. "The Codification of the Law of Territorial Waters," *American Journal of International Law*, XXIV (1930), 486-99.

————. "Submarine and Innocent Passage," *American Journal of International Law*, XI (1917), 147-53.

Smith, H. A. "The Anglo-Norwegian Fisheries Case," *The Year Book of World Affairs* (1953), 283-307.

Sorensen, Max. "Law of the Sea," *International Conciliation*, No. 520 (November, 1958), 195-255.

"Soviet Note of January 7, No. 2/OSA, on the Closing of Peter the Great Bay in Reply to U.S. Protest," *Department of State Bulletin*, XXXVIII (1958), 461-62.

Svarlien, Oscar. "The Territorial Sea: A Quest for Uniformity," *University of Florida Law Review*, XV (1962), 333-51.

Uchida, H. "The Soviet Legal Theory of the Law of the Sea (Sovieto no Kaiyo-ho Riron)," *Legal Reports* (Horitsu Ziho), XXX (1958), 934-39.

"United Nations, Report of the International Law Commission Covering Its Second Session, June 5-July 29, 1950," *American Journal of International Law*, XLIV (1950), 148-60.

"United Nations, Report of the International Law Commission Covering the Work of Its Eighth Session, April 23-July 4, 1956," *American Journal of International Law*, LI (1957), Off. Doc. 154-256.

"U.S. Protests to U.S.S.R. on Closing of Peter the Great Bay," *Department of State Bulletin*, XXXVII (1957), 388.

Vaughan, Robert M. "Delimitation of Norwegian Fisheries Zone," *Geographical Review*, XLII (1952), 302-4.

Waldock, C. H. M. "The Anglo-Norwegian Fisheries Case," *British Yearbook of International Law*, XXVIII (1951), 114-71.

————. "International Law and the New Maritime Claims," *International Relations*, I (1956), 163-94.

Walker, Wyndham L. "Territorial Waters: The Cannon Shot Rule," *British Yearbook of International Law*, XXII (1945), 210-12.

Wilson, George Grafton. "Topic I: Marginal Sea and Other Waters," *International Law Topics and Discussions* (1913), 11-53.

Young, Richard. "The Anglo-Norwegian Fisheries Case," *American Bar Association Journal*, XXXVIII (1952), 243-45.

————. "The Legal Status of Submarine Areas beneath the High Seas," *American Journal of International Law*, XLV (1951), 225-39.

OTHER PERIODICALS AND NEWSPAPERS CITED:

The Christian Science Monitor, 1963.
Inter-American Juridical Yearbook, 1956-1957, 1957.
International Law Situations, United States Naval War College, 1939, 1955, 1956.
The New York Times, 1957-63.
The Report, International Law Association, 1922.
The Times (London), 1952, 1953, 1957-63.

UNIVERSITY OF FLORIDA MONOGRAPHS

Social Sciences